ALEXANDER ARMSTRONG

LAND OF THE MIDNIGHT SUN

MY ARCTIC ADVENTURES

CORGI BOOKS

TRANSWORLD PUBLISHERS
61–63 Uxbridge Road, London W5 5SA
www.transworldbooks.co.uk

Transworld is part of the Penguin Random House group of companies
whose addresses can be found at global.penguinrandomhouse.com

Penguin
Random House
UK

First published in Great Britain in 2015 by Bantam Press
an imprint of Transworld Publishers
Corgi edition published 2016

A CIP catalogue record for this book
is available from the British Library.

ISBN
9780552172011

Typeset in 11.5/15pt Minion by Falcon Oast Graphic Art Ltd.
Printed and bound by Clays Ltd, Bungay, Suffolk.

Penguin Random House is committed to a sustainable
future for our business, our readers and our planet. This book is made from Forest
Stewardship Council® certified paper.

MIX
Paper from
responsible sources
FSC® C018179

1 3 5 7 9 10 8 6 4 2

To Hannah and the boys

Contents

Part Three – The Final Frontier: North American Arctic

Introduction

I have started seeing ghosts. Not everywhere, of course – I'm not weird; just very occasionally in the darker corners of my vision a shape appears that my brain interprets as a person. So far no headless cavaliers, just an endless procession of grey ladies who disappear under closer scrutiny. The ghosts came suddenly; in fact I know the day they arrived, even the hour, and their emergence – which I shall get into shortly – is entirely down to the planning of this Arctic journey.

I first started talking to ITV about the possibility of doing a complete circumnavigation of the Arctic region in the spring of 2014, and the programme was officially commissioned in May that year, just two weeks after my wife and I discovered we would be having another baby (our fourth – I know). The baby was due to arrive in time for Christmas, which is exactly when I was due to be

heading off to the cold. It is some testimony to the for-
bearance and resilience of my wife that I write this
introduction in the summer of 2015 from the warm hearth
of our happy marital home still very much attached to all
those organs a lesser woman might have been tempted to
have on a plate.

The series has been called *Land of the Midnight Sun*,
which I think sounds wonderful. The 24-hour daylight
in northern summertime is just an extraordinary
phenomenon, utterly baffling to us temperate zone
dwellers although not entirely unappealing. On family
holidays to Scotland in August there was always something
stupidly exotic about the persistence of the light up to
midnight – as children we took it as divine justification for
staying up far too late. Despite this title, I am actually
starting my journey in the depths of winter, when the
whole region is in fact blanketed in polar night. But over
the course of the journey, the Arctic rapidly switches
(literally in a matter of weeks) from being permanently
sunless to being in permanent daylight. What a ringside
seat I will get for this little trick, and seeing what effect it
has on us all.

I don't think I'm alone in nursing deep, almost atavistic,
feelings about the extreme cold regions of the world. There
is something so inviting about nature in its coldest state.
There's not a landscape or vista on the planet that doesn't
look ten times more enticing hung about with snow and
crisp with ice. But the allure goes beyond the mere
picturesque; I think – fanciful nonsense though it sounds

– that we're nicer people in the cold. Seriously. It's no coincidence that Christmas is known as the season of goodwill. It is in our nature to gather together in the cold, for reasons of instinctive economy if one wants to be pragmatic about it, to preserve and perpetuate body heat like the emperor penguins (I know, I know, NOT in the Arctic). And the beauty of a snow-bound wintery scene comes hand-in-hand with this implicit sense of heightened comradeship: what schmaltzy Christmas cards like to call 'good cheer'.

Yes, this may amount to nothing more than the sharing of warmth and victuals, but coming as I do from a temperate zone of the globe, I find that overwhelmingly appealing – even mystically so. Notice how often we use words like 'magical' to describe winter scenery (which itself of course is a 'wonderland') in a way we never would a summer landscape. And we're not wrong: sending things sub-zero casts an instant spell on nature. This, I reckon, is why we all trog off skiing in our droves. I'm not saying that sliding down hills isn't fun in itself but being somewhere so thoroughly wintery is sublime. Throw in log fires and several jugs of mulled wine and you begin to see my point, surely. Put it this way, if the Disney film had been called *Scorched* I doubt very much there would be a million children in the world singing 'Let It Go!' at any given moment.

I, however, have never been further north than Stornoway, so have long been hankering after an excuse to go up to the proper North, to meet the people, first those of our continent up in Scandinavia, then out across the wider Arctic. I've longed to see the Lands of the Midnight Sun (for there are many), to watch icebergs drift across bays, to stand in solitude beneath the Northern Lights, to walk across glaciers, to ski across majestic icy wastes, and then come in each night to a roaring fire and cosy glass or two in excellent company. And this was surely the trip to do all of those things.

It's a lovely thing to be in that TV grey area of Having Once Been A Sketch Comedy Performer. Had I gone off into my own little sideline of practising obstetrics, manufacturing stairlifts or training racehorses, I daresay I'd have been released from the duty of care that the industry (very decently) feels it has towards me. But I'm afraid I haven't; I've just hung around on the sidelines of TV like one of those people that won't leave a party (my mother's rather brilliant trick with them, incidentally, is just to say 'I think we might all now say a prayer' and they're gone in seconds flat), and so therefore I'm in line for the glorious treats that get lobbed out occasionally. As a comedian, one is supposed to have the requisite balance of curiosity, bonhomie and scepticism that make one the perfect stand-in for all the millions of people who are better qualified to front television documentaries. And 'Amen' I say to that.

The trip was ultimately scaled (very slightly) down to a journey from Norway (up near the Russian border in the east, just a stone's throw from Murmansk) round to Alaska (up near the Russian border in the west, just a stone's throw from Siberia). That is to say we covered the entire

Arctic Circle apart from Russia. Russia's Arctic region was deemed simply too mind-warpingly enormous for us to be able to encompass it in this particular tale. Perhaps one day I will get to put in that missing piece of the puzzle.

One of the things I discovered during our Arctic preparations was that we could expect to be at temperatures below −40° Celsius, at which point the tears in your eyes start to freeze. As a contact-lens wearer of some years' standing, I asked if lenses were practicable and was told roundly 'No, they aren't', so I went for the nuclear option and had – not laser surgery, which, as is well known, is for wusses, but – lens implants. This involved my own lenses being whipped out of my eyes and synthetic Carl Zeiss lenses being put in in their stead. So, yes, I now have German eyes. And thanks to their rather beautiful design these new lenses throw strange concentric light refractions on to my retina from time to time, and it is this that has created the strange spectral figures on the edge of my vision.

I suppose the relationship between my optic nerve and my brain has been so good till now that the brain just takes everything the former offers it on trust. If there's the merest mischief of a shape on the periphery, then – no questions asked – the brain will ordain that it is most likely a person, or a thing, or a . . . oh, hang on, it's gone. And so I now have to live with the possibility that all these chimeras are actual things (right up until the moment they vanish) and hope that my brain learns to recalibrate before too long.

This journal of my Arctic travels occasionally suffers from the same effect. I am no expert on the wider Arctic region; I am only really able to write about the experience of following the particular narrow path I took through it. But, occasionally, little eddies on the periphery of that narrow journey get blown into subjects on which I have very little authority to speak, yet somehow feel perfectly entitled to bang on about. Please overlook these moments – I hope they're rare – and accept my apologies.

Thank you very much. I now leave you entering the Arctic Circle somewhere in Norway . . .

Part One

Nice on Ice: Scandinavia

1

Do You Come Here Lofoten?

It's early February and Day One finds me arriving in Bodø, the capital of the Northern Norwegian county of Nordland (just in case there's any doubt about which point of the compass we've been following to get here). It's about halfway up the country, pushing north, on the narrowest strip. It is reassuringly cold, which is terrific, as that was the first Arctic novelty I had been looking forward to experiencing, and, yes, just a couple of feet outside the cosy interior of the Norwegian Air fuselage, there it is: The Cold. On first impact not noticeably colder than the surprising chill I've often felt stepping off the train at Newcastle Central on a winter's evening, but a good deal more aggressive. This is a temperature that, were it stepping off the train at Newcastle, would be heading straight down the Bigg Market in its finest Friday-night vest, looking for trouble. By the time I get to the bottom of the steps, I am pulling fistfuls of everything out of my rucksack. Somewhere in there amongst my spare thermals, my water bottle, my crampons, my head-torch, my survival blanket, my emergency bothy (a sort of flat, folded Wendy house of thick polythene to which I might owe my life AT ANY STAGE), my spare bars of chocolate, my nice Williamson tea from home, my extra-thick spare socks, my hand warmers, my spare batteries for the head-torch, my Blisteze, my Gore-tex rain-hood-y thing, my compass, somewhere there must be my gloves, my hat, my scarf, anything . . .

Yes, there's nothing polite about this climate; it is, just so we can be absolutely clear on this point, insistently cold. However, I have a bigger concern at this juncture. I have spent an entire day now, from the moment we all checked in at Gatwick at starling's parp this morning, in the care of Norwegians, and I am beginning to spot some alarming consistencies among them. In fact by now, well into the evening, I am quite certain there is something rum afoot: a very troubling conspiracy. They are all actively genial, and in one or two particularly worrying instances they have even gone out of their way to help us. It is all deeply suspect. So far 100 per cent of the Norwegians I have met have been 'lovely'. It's as if just before I've turned each corner they've come whooping and high-fiving out of a huddle in which they've been focusing on how they, as a people, can polish their interpersonal skills till you can't look at them with the naked eye.

Is this a weather thing? Do they feel they have to atone

for the intransigence of their climate? Or maybe they get so used to having to change their plans every hour of the day to make the best of whatever's thrown down on them that they're just inherently easy-going. I am determined to get to the bottom of it. When we turned up in Oslo with a hundred massive flight cases and wanted to check them in for a connecting flight that didn't leave for seven hours (we had quite a lot of that – Norwegian Air's schedules are clearly drawn up by a Brit), they had the effrontery to say 'OK!' and then be funny, even charming. In English. It is almost like they are showing off, and I can't begin to tell you how annoying it is. I ask if anyone else in our party has noticed this whole-nation-of-Norwegian-people-being-nice thing, and it seems the others have picked up on it too. In fact it turns out they're renowned for it; Norwegians are the second happiest race in the world after the Danes. Of course that sounds like the kind of terrible old bollocks that fills the middle pages of Sunday tabloids until I tell you that this is according to a survey by the United Nations General Assembly. The top nine are: Denmark, Norway, Switzerland, the Netherlands, Sweden, Canada, Finland, Austria and Iceland. Now, if I were a maverick detective inspector and I'd written that little list down in my notebook, I reckon I wouldn't even have got through my fourth pint in the picturesque pub before the eureka moment came: all those countries are cold – some of them get famously snowbound. There simply has to be a link between happiness and the cold. Barman, another pint of heavy, please.

What is it about these Norwegians? Well, I've already spotted two things. They eat an awful lot of fish and they sound like Geordies. No, really they do, and as a Northumbrian I can't tell you how comforting that is. If I blur my hearing (don't tell me you don't know how to do that – didn't you ever have a *Magic Ear* book in the nineties?), the hurdy-gurdy inflection and ümläütёd vowels of Norwegian suddenly transform into the beautiful 'Eeeeeeh Aa knooooow' of home. I might be back on the Morpeth bus. But perhaps even more pertinently they are, as a people, astonishingly rich. Their mineral wealth is something they don't like to boast about – preferring to spend it very sensibly on ethical invest-ments for future generations rather than hosing it up the wall in London's glitzy nightspots. Or at least if they do they're being extremely discreet about it. Put it this way, I've certainly never seen a Lamborghini with the number plate 'Morten 1' hooning it down Park Lane in a blizzard of Class As and East European hookers, but maybe I just haven't been looking hard enough.

Our first evening in Bodø (this incidentally is not pro-nounced to rhyme with 'Frodo', which my Norwegian interlocutors found hilarious, but rather more with 'murder', which, appropriately, is what I was committing on their tongue) is spent as I hope many subsequent nights will be – having an extremely convivial time eating baked cod in a rough wood-panelled restaurant about a quarter of a mile's slither along the ice slab from our hotel.

The very first outing of the series to capture that exciting

First Shot Of The Series – always a symbolic and nervy experience presenting for the first time with a new crew and new director – takes us to the military end of the airport at Bodø (is this something all airports have?). We are going to be flying up out of the airport in a little twin prop on a round trip so that we can catch the very moment of my crossing the Arctic Circle and coming in to land. I don't know how I'm feeling about this – I'm going to say 'excited', but, having never been up in a small aircraft before, there's a tiny bit of 'bricking it' in there too. It's a bit like that moment where you've paid for your ride at the fair and now you're just sitting waiting for it to start and you've noticed that all the other passengers are teenage boys.

We're ushered into one of the huge half-submerged hangars that crouch up by the military end like lots of mini Gateshead Sages built of reinforced concrete. They each have terrifying 60-tonne steel doors that open outwards on vast hinges like the lids of giant pedal bins sleeping off a binge. The hangars were originally built to house single NATO jet fighters in those crazy Cold War days of the 1980s. Nowadays our one looks like any non-military aircraft hangar anywhere in the known world: a hotchpotch of maybe seven or eight small aircraft, some with missing bits, some under tarpaulins; piles of tools (religiously ranked and filed in gleaming order), spare parts, broken kettles and buggered armchairs with what appear to be Don King's barber sweepings bursting out of them here and there.

A crisp and alert fellow called Jon is introduced to me. He, I'm delighted to say, is my pilot and not the stout man next to him breathing through his mouth, with the untucked shirt and the cold sore. Jon and his friend drag out two planes (one for me, one for Rog the cameraman) on the campest, dinkiest little trolley you've ever seen, which attaches on to the front wheel of the plane. Never has a tool so undersung its role – it's like watching Ben Whishaw rip up a phonebook. When all is ready, Jon and I climb into the cockpit and by now I've already seen and heard enough to know that he too is part of the Norwegian Conspiracy. He is an exceedingly nice person. I recoil and shudder inwardly.

Having never been 'up front' on a plane, I've never witnessed the catechism of pre-take-off procedure before, so I can't say if this is normal, but Jon has a laminated card in front of him and as he goes down the forty or so bullet points thereon, he reads them aloud in English (for my benefit?) and checks the corresponding dials and switches and coils and glitter-drops (I think that's right). After about seven minutes, during which time the props have been started up (first the starboard, then the port) and seemingly every one of the 120 knobs and breakers in front of us has been switched, turned or caressed, Jon says we're ready to go, reassuring me that the heating will be turned on as soon as we are in the air. I hadn't even noticed till now that I am shivering with cold. God, yes, it's freezing. Of course. I was so transfixed by the excitement of leaving the ground in this tiny bit of fibreglass that I hadn't been checking up on my thermostat. Wow – I've got my big gloves on and my fingers are about to drop off. Jon says something friendly in Norwegian to the control tower, who in turn say something delightful back, Jon wangs up the throttle and we blast (not very far) down the runway before lifting blithely up into the snowy heavens. We're off!

When my brother, sister and I were little, we used to have something that we called, for some reason, The Bogey. It was basically just an old-fashioned pram base that we'd found in the garage. We would sit on it at the top of the hill on our quiet single-track road, whoever was at the front would steer by manoeuvring my father's old sack trolley to the left or right with their feet (my idea that, remarkably effective) and off we'd fly down the hill into any oncoming traffic (happily rare) with the wind and midges in our hair. There were no brakes, so if a car did come along or you needed to stop urgently for whatever reason you just had to swerve the trolley off into the hedge and hope the pram base would follow (it DID!) and it wouldn't hurt too much (it DID!). The Bogey's time came to an abrupt end, though, not as it happens in a smash-up or a delicate sack-trolley-being-extracted-from-child A&E trip. But because some passer-by came to the door one day when it was just me at home and asked if they could have the pram base. And being only eight and rather a drip, I hadn't really learnt to say 'no' to grown-ups, so off it went in the back of some-one's car. I was so distraught I could barely get the words out to tell my parents when they got back.

Aaaaaanyway, the incredibly dull point you can probably sense I'm about to make is that nothing I've ever been on or in has ever given me the madly exciting sense of propulsion I got from walloping down the hill on The Bogey. Until being in the cockpit of a twin prop. That is the closest thing to having wings of your own. It's possibly the noise, or the thinness of the membrane between you and the sky outside, or maybe it's the fact that you can see and feel the instant effect of every control the pilot touches, but this is a million miles away from strapping yourself into Row 12 in an Airbus. This reminds you how thrillingly unlikely the laws of aerodynamics are when seen up close. The temptation to shout 'Wheeeeeeeeee!' is impossible to ignore . . .

Bodø slides away beneath us, jets of warm air start very obligingly to curl into the corners of the cabin and spread their goodness, and then without a moment's warning Jon passes me the controls.

'It's quite complicated,' he tells me. 'Push to go down, pull to go up, turn to the right to go to the right and to the left to go left. You think you can remember that?'

He shows me the two dials I have to watch for altitude and bearing, and I try not to grip the joystick too hard. I've steered plenty of boats before so can keep a steady course when right and left are the only options, but it's this up and down business that's going to be the problem here. Sure enough, we immediately start drifting quite high above the ceiling height Jon has recommended, so under his instruction I gently move the joystick forwards. The plane lurches down, and even though it's my hand on the controls my stomach freefalls away to my knees.

'A bit more gently,' says Jon, a bit more gently than I would have said it.

I ease the joystick towards me, and the plane swoops back up like a flush going round a U-bend. I don't feel especially scared, as Jon has a joystick in front of him too and can take over the second anything goes woefully wrong (he doesn't), but I do get a strong sense that if I had ever thought of flying as just 'driving in the sky', then I may have overlooked certain complexities. Jon then instructs me to bring the plane around in a wide arc, so I turn the wheel (I bet it's not called a wheel) and sure enough the starboard wing dips down rather exhilaratingly, and the crew behind me (the film crew; we didn't opt for cabin crew) start to tighten their grips on the armrests. I'm quite grateful when Jon offers to take back the controls for the return to Bodø, but my relief subsides after about five seconds into a feverish need to DO IT AGAIN. Sadly we're on a tight schedule and have to get ourselves de-rigged and off to the ferry port in time for the last boat to Moskenes, so my pilot's licence will have to wait. Interestingly, just as we land, the roar of seven fighter jets taking off puts me right on a small historical inaccuracy: turns out the Cold War hasn't finished – it's just moved to a hangar further down the runway.

We hop on to the ferry to Moskenes in the Lofoten Islands – about 100 km northwards from Bodø – at 3 p.m. Embarkation is a very informal affair – a world away from boarding the Townsend Thoresen at Stranraer. In Norway you simply amble on to the boat at any moment up until the very last, whereupon you are given the kind of unmarried-billionaire-uncle welcome that makes you wonder if perhaps the crew have confused you with someone else. But, no, this is repeated for every single party that strides up the gangplank. I do wonder if I'll ever get used to the cussed loveliness of these Devil-forsaken people.

We disgorge from the ferry at what feels like midnight but is in fact only 7 p.m. (this is the inevitable effect of it turning dark not long after lunchtime). We drive the short distance to Leknes, where our hotel is to be found. After the pleasing functionality of our Bodø accommodation, this has the soul-sapping appearance of a place that, were it in the UK, would make you want to examine your life and make binding promises to yourself that you would 'never do this again'. It's an industrial barn on two floors with tiny little cells off a central corridor that are essentially storage lock-ups. I have a brief but potent bout of home-ward yearning and then things quickly start to pick up. Because even here in the most God-awful surroundings, the preternatural warmth of these people shines through. Yes, we seem to be penned for a couple of nights in the sort of place you'd more normally expect to bump into an antique dealer locking up his Chippendales, but the family who run this place go so many extra miles to make it lovely that I end up rather feeling huge affection for it.

For example, screening off part of the reception area is

a rather chic row of white-painted tongue and groove panels behind which is one of the friendliest restaurants you could hope to find anywhere. There's a cluster of maybe seven or eight tables each decorated with flowers and little night-light candles, and the whole thing is served by just one single chef, who can be seen and heard cheerfully cooking everything to order, and a wonderfully dry, deadpan and very pregnant waitress. ('Well, I hope you like cod and reindeer.' Why, what's on the menu? 'Cod, reindeer, or I suppose you could have cod and reindeer.' As it happens we badly wanted cod and reindeer, and both were ambrosial.) I like to think the chef and the waitress were an item, as that would just complete the idyll for me, although it is entirely possible that they weren't and merely worked together – I'm aware this does also sometimes happen. It was so cheering to find that even here in this unlikely place there were so many personal touches, so many instances of someone doing something just because it struck them as being a nice thing to do, that my momentary homesickness was banished. We even tried to make reservations for the following night. The waitress thought that was hilarious ('I don't think it will be necessary').

The Lofoten Islands themselves are famous for many things, chiefly their beauty. You'll never find a more pleasing rugged-coastline-and-soaring-mountains combination. But just a couple of clicks behind the beauty come the celebrated Lofoten fish. The islands are a kind of lush Eden for the codfish – albeit the kind of lush Eden from which some of their number are routinely plucked and served up on a plate. But the long and the short of it is that every year the world's largest cod shoal (indeed the planet's only growing cod stock) drops by for the famous 'skrei' season. By virtue of the happy confluence of the Gulf Stream and inch-perfect submarine direction-finding, each February millions of these wonderful fish swim here all the way from the Barents Sea, over a thousand kilometres away, in the hope of getting lucky, which, judging by the statistics, pretty much all of them do – it's essentially Club 18–30 for our scaly friends. And thanks to the Norwegians' innate knack for practical forward thinking, they have never fished the things to extinction – *au contraire*, they have caught them through patient line fishing, always being particularly strict on themselves to respect their quotas, never taking more than is sustainable.

The way the shoal has grown and grown over the centuries remains an exquisite if rare example of man and nature living in per-fect har-mo-nee. Man protects the shoal and its breeding grounds and, in exchange, can take a healthy proportion of the fish therein. As ever, man gets the better half of this deal and STILL – in other parts of the world at least – his greed gets the better of him and he ends up cocking it all up. Not here, though. Not in Norway. I am beginning to wonder if this curious agreeableness I keep coming across here mightn't actually spring from genuine decency. It's still just a theory at this stage, but it's not entirely out of the question.

* * *

We have arrived in the Lofoten Islands at the very beginning of the skrei season. In fact that's nonsense, we have arrived at what should be the beginning of the skrei season. We are due to go out to sea with Børge, a fine fellow with twinkly eyes and a beard and a voice like tearing metal, who has been fishing from the village of Ballstad all his life. His father fished in Ballstad before him and both his grandfathers before that. He didn't provide any further lineage, but I'll eat my hat if any of his great-grandparents were quantity surveyors. He also has a son who has fished with him since boyhood. Oh, so that's good, your son will take over the family fishing business one day? 'No,' says Børge. 'He's going to work in the oil industry – they will pay him twice as much as I can, hahahaha.' If there's a trace of rancour in this answer, Børge keeps it well hidden behind bravura cheerfulness and a hard, film-star smile.

The very words Fishing Village magic up an impossibly romantic tableau, don't they? We may picture something Cornish or something like our lovely Craster in Northumberland, built out of dark coastal whinstone, dotted about with lobster pots and bobbing fishing boats, where hardbitten sea swains go out in the middle of the night risking their necks to bring in their haul, while salty old men and women with pipes sit on the pier and mend nets or dress crabs and perhaps a man with anchor tattoos plays shanties on a squeeze-box. The whole scene, slightly soft focused at the edges now I look more closely, is scented with oak smoke from the smokery and seaweed from the foreshore (a blend I was brought up to recognize as being

'Ozone' – which we're now told is complete rubbish: the air at the coast is apparently no richer in oxygen than anywhere else. Ah well . . .). In truth our fishing industry, sometimes because its hands are tied by the quotas of the EU's Common Fisheries Policy, sometimes because the enormous shoals are no longer there, hasn't really got enough going on to support the communities that once thrived on it, so the shanty-man (if he ever existed) is now an estate agent in Fulham and the net-menders run an amusement arcade where the Plymouth Brethren hut used to be, the villages are full of holiday cottages that sit empty for much of the year and those few boats that do go out have little choice but to take an industrial approach to their fishing. The CFP's fish quotas, however well intentioned, haven't done anything to halt the decline in fishing stocks. Huge numbers of fish are still caught, only to be thrown back into the sea dead.

Ballstad, however, is the very acme of fishing villages. You only have to look at the gleaming factories on the quayside that process the thousands and thousands of tons of fish that come through every day to know how well it does from its industry. Ballstad is also very beautiful – one might almost call it a fishing resort: all pastel-coloured villas and beautifully kept painted wooden houses. This happy community is completely supported by a sustainable natural resource at its heart. It does make you wonder what it would take to get British fisheries back to this state or if that's even possible. Craster happens to be going through a purple patch thanks to the enormous popularity of its kippers, but for many of our other fishing communities it's just been decade after decade of steady decline.

We meet Børge at the fishery at 5 a.m. in order to join his early-morning outing to check on his lines. The boat is a smallish one with a modest wheelhouse and a deep hull into which all the catch will be thrown. Børge had been out fishing just the evening before and says the skrei still hadn't arrived then. There had been some cod in his catch but nothing like the quantities he will see once the season has started in earnest. The boat has an unsurprising tang of fish about it but nothing like as back-of-the-throat yacky as I was expecting. I suppose the fact that it is in constant use and the fact that it is freezing bloody cold keeps it from becoming toxically fishy. A fishmonger opened up on our walk to school a couple of years ago, which changed our lives and hugely improved our diet; they had the most beautiful silvery bounty spread out each day on the ice. But you really wouldn't want a fish shop to open up next door or, worse still, beneath you. They were meticulous about scouring the shop each evening with disinfectant and scrubbing the pavement outside, but still you always held your breath when you walked past.

Callum, our sound guy, spent several weeks on the trawlers filming a series for the BBC, and I notice he heads straight for the deck of Børge's boat and doesn't dare venture down below even once, the combination of swell and smell, I guess, just brings back too many gorge-raising memories for him. We pull out of the harbour and on to the flat sea beyond. There is a gentle rise and fall but nothing too unsettling, Callum still looks fairly hale. Børge shows me below to the galley where all the kit is kept, and digs around for some overalls and trousers in my size and a pair of enormous fishy gauntlets.

Børge doesn't speak superb English, but his trademark '*Ja! Ja!*' is delivered with such a slow and winning inflection – and at such a high decibel level – that it's hard not to think he's somehow sending himself up. He has something Tom Waits-like about him, something granite-edged. Come to think of it, the cod themselves also have little Tom Waits tufts growing just below their mouths. That must be the reason I've somehow got the lyrics of 'Shore Leave' going round my head . . .

Børge ordains it is time for coffee (he seems to have had a cup on the go since we arrived, but I'll certainly not say no). Børge drinks out of the same coffee cup from season's start to its end and tells me proudly that he NEVER WASHES IT UP. I'm not sure if this is down to superstition, like an actor talking about his lucky socks, or pragmatism simply because the cup is never really out of use for long enough to warrant a proper clean. But I say 'Wow' in response, which I think just about covers both contexts.

Certainly Børge puts the hours in on the water – apparently over four thousand of them a year (he points to the wheelhouse tachograph as he says this, so, although I don't inspect it to verify, I take him at his word). Each evening he splutters out across the bay to lay up to 7 km of lines with baited hooks. He puts a buoy at each end of them and marks them up on the swish electronic chart on his computer so that by the time he's finished the screen shows seven or eight thin scraggy lines in parallel, as if the sea has wrinkled like Cornelius the Elephant. Then each morning he heads back out for ten hours to pull them all in. He's usually on his own – the boat is set up to run as a one-man show – and I can readily picture him at his wheel in all weathers and at all times of day and night, shouting '*Ja! Ja!*' at the horizon, a flinty smile on his face, a filthy mug in his hand: a supremely happy man.

We start winching in the lines. The key thing about line fishing is that only a tiny sliver of the shoal is caught, a minute fraction of a per cent, so there's none of the indiscriminate blanket hoover-up that you get with netting. Also, each fish is taken from the line by hand, so if any are undersize they get thrown straight back to live for another day. It's the difference between picking ripe apples from a tree over a season as and when they are ready and coming along with a dirty great machine that rips the entire tree out of the ground and shakes all the apples, ripe or not, into a pile to be sorted later. After fairly inauspicious beginnings, more and more cod start coming in over the side, one or two of them by no means small. Then there's one that Børge estimates to be about 30 kilos. If it's over 30 kilos, then it'll win Børge a kilo of coffee back in Ballstad. This elicits a broad grin from the man of the sea, and he announces sheepishly that maybe the skrei season has just started after all.

What, I wonder, will happen to these beautifully maintained habitats without future generations of Børges tending them so carefully? What if the next generation brings in bigger ships or introduces a more industrial means of extraction? I suppose, as long as it's the Norwegians in charge, the cod stocks should be in safe hands, but the allure of heavy industry's big money, the kind that is drawing Børge's son away from his birthright, does seem to be such an unstoppable force. You can't help wondering how these fragile and beautiful quid pro quos with nature can possibly survive against the seemingly unarguable arithmetic of the wad.

We chug back to Ballstad with the ship's belly full of fish and find that news of Børge's whopper has brought a man from the local paper to the dockside with the kilo of coffee to hand over if the cod weighs in over the magic 30 kilos. The scales say 33 kilos and so Børge is being photographed with his enormous bag of coffee and a crinkly smile as we say our goodbyes and head off on our journey back to the mainland by road.

Driving in the Arctic, in case you're wondering, is a good deal less perilous than you might expect. Yes, the road surface is invariably compacted snow and ice, but all the tyres are fitted with studs and this makes an astonishing difference. They won't keep you from careening out alarmingly on corners, though; so far we've missed the thundering juggernauts coming the other way, but if we did happen to be in their path I can't help wondering how much they'd be able to do to avoid us. Best not think about that, eh?

We travel in two vehicles: the hero car ('hero' is a curious film expression that simply means 'it will appear on screen'. So on film units you hear questions like 'Could we have the hero coffee on set, please?', which results in a beautiful porcelain cup and saucer of hot coffee being produced, not from catering but from the props department – it may easily not be entirely potable), which is the car I am seen driving around on the show, and the camera van that contains the thousand flight cases holding all the camera and sound equipment. Dom our director and I share the driving duties in the first car, and it has become an early custom of ours to tune in to the very local-est of the local radio stations we can find. We have only been in Norway for two days and already a couple of Scandi pop classics are worming their way into our souls. Strangely, even as you drive through the most mountainous passes of Northern Norway, the radio signal stays remarkably constant. If this were the north of Scotland, the plangent chorus of '*Styggen På Ryggen*' would ebb and flow some-what with the topography, but the Norwegians have clearly opted for a strength of signal to suit their landscape. Again, I find that eerily impressive.

The camera van contains Rog the cameraman and Callum (whom we've already met), and Hermione our assistant producer. By and large we drive in convoy, although I notice Rog – in common with nearly every cameraman I've ever met – seems to have the very latest and most sophisticated apps and gizmos, including in this case one for navigation, so he frequently arrives at our destinations way ahead of us as he's not reliant on whatever crappy satnav we have. I am becoming used to the 'Up and Past' shot, which is what Rog demands every time the roads take a turn for the prettier. Either a cracking view or the light on a distant mountain will catch Rog's eye and he'll get us to stop so he can jump out and film me driving past several times in different sizes of shot and on different lenses. These visuals are the bread and butter of documentary making as they can sit very usefully under voiceover or a bit of stirring music and they keep the thing ticking along, telling the story of our progress all the while. At one point we stop at the side of the road in the middle of nowhere, not realizing that we are completely blocking the entrance to someone's drive. Rather embarrassingly they turn up while we're there, but whereas in England we might expect a testily wound-down window and 'Can I help you?!', in Norway we are greeted by a lovely couple of men (again, I assume they're an item . . .) who want to know if there's anything they can do for us. Are we OK? Do we need any help? Can they supply us with anything? Tea? Coffee? Biscuits? A tow? No, we say, we're fine, thank you! Although it turns out we absolutely do need a tow, as my right-hand wheels have completely sunk into the verge.

And a biscuit too, actually.

2

The Ice Hotel: A Stupendous Cathedral of 'Brrrr'

Just because we are driving on northwards from Leknes I have somehow got it into my head that Harstad, our next destination, will be another tiny settlement by the fjord. My internal logic seems to have decided that conurbations at this northerly latitude are completely out of the question. But, no, I couldn't be more wrong. Harstad is an enormous place. It's also home to a Royal Marines Arctic Training Centre, which is where we are to spend the following day.

We had done a day of Arctic Training back in London about three weeks before we left, on a nippy January afternoon, but as this had involved us sitting around eating creamy biscuits in an ITV meeting room, there hadn't really been an especially strong practical element to it. On that occasion the training was provided by the excellent Paul Mattin, an ex-Major in the Marines, who spent the day plying us with cautionary tales of sub-zero derring-do (many – in fact now I come to think of it, all – of them starring Paul Mattin, an ex-Major in the Marines) and showing us slides of a recent Antarctic trip with his buddies, including some quite personal ones ('Look away, ladies') of what can happen when you expose your extremities to extreme cold. Paul had said that our trip was going to be 'gnarly – [with a meaningful look around the table] very gnarly indeed'.

Extreme weather training is one of the cornerstones of Marine discipline and preparation – their traditional strong suit is Arctic and Mountain Warfare, and so it seems only right that they should come here to learn it rather than Antigua, say (or in front of a plate of biscuits in an air-conditioned meeting room on London's South Bank). We're here to be put through the equivalent of Day One on their training programme: a crash course in survival, focusing on warmth, shelter and food. Not just for fun, you understand, as there's every chance we might find ourselves 'benighted' (as ex-Major in the Marines Paul Mattin delights in saying instead of 'forced to stay out all night'). No one gives better instruction than an army NCO. I suppose that shouldn't really be surprising; it's a skill that's passed down from generation to generation. But beneath that bluff mixture of bravado, step-by-step procedure and hur-hurrh-hurrh army wit is a ruthlessly efficient teaching system. Never have I witnessed such attention focused on a trainer's every word, but then all these soldiers are about to go out and spend five days in the wild at sub-zero. There's nothing like imminent practical submersion to focus the mind.

The fire-lighting course holds few surprises except for the exciting revelation that cotton wool is highly flammable (who knew?) and never more so than when smothered in lip-salve (wahey!). The food course is significantly gingered up by the arrival of live hens, of which we are then instructed in the humane killing. The Marine corporal gives us a practical demo of how to put a live chicken at its ease, how to lay it down with its neck sticking out, how to put a stout stick across the neck and then, with a sharp tug, how you can quickly turn the closest living relation to the dinosaurs into something delicious and sustaining. You've always got to be a bit careful on telly about not upsetting people or indeed putting yourself in the firing line for the pitchfork-and-torch processions that seemingly sane people like to visit on anyone who gets involved in the process of turning animals into meat (which so many of us cheerfully eat). God knows how all this'll look on the flat screen in the corner of the sitting room, but if it never makes it into the prog you'll know exactly why. I get selected by the food man to skin the chicken and 'dress' it (a very polite way of saying 'remove the guts'), which is immediately followed by our lunch. I scrub my hands as well as I can with some snow, but for obvious reasons this is a fairly cursory business. Then I get stuck into the sandwiches.

I leave the Harstad base strangely disappointed that the day hasn't involved me being shouted at by pink-faced men with close-cropped ginger hair only inches from my face while I do press-ups in the snow. Or rather, I leave the base wondering how much more satisfying it would be if that were the kind of day I was driving away from. However, I have learnt how to build a brush shelter with a roaring log fire and to make a chicken stew from an exceedingly fresh bird, so that was nice. Best of all, though, was the welcome appearance of ex-Major in the Marines Paul Mattin, who had somehow talked his way into a Harstad trip to coincide with ours. While the crew had gone off in the afternoon to get general shots of the camp, Paul and I had found ourselves back in our natural habitat, the meeting room, getting stuck into yet another exercise with creamy biscuits.

Among the many things Paul Mattin had passed on to us during our previous intensive biscuit day was the extremely welcome news that we should abandon any thoughts of a post-Christmas diet; on the contrary, he said we should be bulking up on carbs ('Lean into it, men' were his exact words). We would be burning up nigh on 9,000 calories a day during our time in the Arctic – just trying to keep our bodies warm – and so now was not a time for holding back. And I can tell you that if I did nothing else Paul told me, I followed this instruction to the letter. Almost a week into the trip, however, I do begin to wonder at the differences between ex-Major in the Marines Paul Mattin's imagining of our trip and . . . our trip, because we don't appear to be spending our days and nights dancing with danger out on the Arctic tundra. So far I haven't found any of the Scandic hotels we've been staying in particularly 'gnarly'. Admittedly the tea selection in my room the night before last didn't include Earl Grey, but these are the sorts of hardships I have been preparing myself for on this once-in-a-lifetime Arctic journey. If the great Norwegian explorer Roald Amundsen and illustrious Viking wanderer forebears such as Erik the Red could get by with only the most limited range of Twinings products, I don't see why I shouldn't manage it too. And it's in this vein of Heroic Acts of Self-Denial that I've resolved to dial down my food intake a bit. I don't think any of the party has noticed yet, but as of this morning I've decided not to eat the breakfast of three men and the lunch of twelve, because I've noticed that those calories aren't really getting the call-up. This will all change I'm sure, as we get colder and more active, but for now I'm at peak fatness and something must be done.

From Harstad we drive on to Narvik. This should have been an easy three-hour jaunt, but we join an enormous queue of stationary traffic just four miles outside Narvik and there we sit for a further three and a half hours. In our car the local radio station provides a bit of diversion until – possibly as retribution for my part in the chicken slaughter earlier, or at least for my less than clinical handwashing after it – I am suddenly visited by the most horrific stomach cramps, resulting in several trips into the woods with my paper hankies, and some fun new landmarks for tomorrow's dog walkers. Finally, though, having 'made like the bears', I feel I've done something Mattin would be proud of, something he would recognize as being proper survival behaviour.

The traffic jam is all down to an overturned car about two miles ahead of us, but as there are no alternative routes (it's rather like driving on a little island: there's only one road, and it's the wiggly one that goes everywhere) we all just have to sit (and walk and crouch for the lucky ones) it out.

Narvik is the northernmost port in Norway – and famously the only deep-sea port in the Scandinavian Arctic to remain ice free throughout the year. This distinction has made Narvik strategically vital to the Norwegians (and financially, one imagines, splendidly relaxed), as it means that the colossal iron-ore extraction just over the border at Kiruna in Sweden can be shipped from there all year round. Such useful attributes can come at a terrible price, though. Poor Narvik was the scene of vicious fighting in 1940 as Hitler went all out to bring Norway to heel (and get his hands on the iron ore, no doubt). Certainly the old town was completely destroyed by a series of battles that raged between April and June that year.

We travel by train along the iron-ore line over the Swedish border to Kiruna. This is said to be one of the most beautiful train journeys in the world, and they're not wrong. Better still, we travel the route under the care of Bertel, a train conductor by vocation but also a contortionist of accommodation, so far did he bend over backwards to help us. Shortly before we leave, for example, he asks if we'd like to film the train departing (to which our answer is of course YES), so he duly sets up a sizzling shot of himself waving his green flag, blowing his whistle and hopping into his van as the great engine pulls out of the station ten minutes before its official departure time. It stops about 300 yards down the track and dutifully reverses back into Narvik station, but presumably not before several bladders in the waiting room have suddenly felt curiously and urgently full.

But all this was merely by way of hors d'oeuvre in terms of Bertel's magnanimity. He sits down with us at the end of a carriage (that he has kept clear especially for us and our thousand cases). 'Tell me exactly what you want from this journey and I will do my best to sort it out,' he says. So we explain the kind of things we need, and he nods vigorously. At two or three points on the journey he stops the train right there on its track just so we can climb out and film some of his choicest views – once at the head of the fjord, where the train is reversed and driven past the cameras, and again so the iron-ore train from Kiruna with its fifty-eight trucks can thunder by, bang on cue, on the other side.

As part of our kit on this project we have two different drone 'copter cameras. One is massive, with six propellers, and can carry a huge gimballed camera that is controlled by the operator. The smaller one with four props takes a tiny GoPro camera, but both are capable of capturing the most glorious aerial shots that would previously only have been possible with a helicopter. We dispatch the GoPro on this occasion, which soars up above us till it's far out of sight, sending back to the monitor the kind of footage that makes a cameraman go giddy and cry for his mother.

Kiruna, our destination in Sweden, is on the site of an ancient Sami settlement, but the modern town wasn't founded till 1900. The Samis are the indigenous people of that area of Norway, Sweden, Finland and the Kola Peninsula of Russia that sometimes gets called Lapland (note to self: Lapland is a cultural area and not a sovereign state that is recognized by the UN as a nation in its own right beginning with 'L' just in case Osman ever asks me . . .). We might once have called them Lapps, but that term is now to be avoided, as the Samis (as they prefer to be called) regard it as pejorative. Fair enough. The Samis, who've been living in this region semi-nomadically for over twelve thousand years, minding their own business (literally – they've herded reindeer and fished and been perfectly self-sufficient), have been bullied terribly one way or another by the dominant cultures of mainland Europe over the centuries, suffering the worst kinds of ethnic cleansing right up to the middle of the twentieth century. They are now recognized and protected in Norway, Finland and Sweden (not so much on the Kola Peninsula . . .) and have their own parliament, which feels like a step in the right direction, although strangely it doesn't seem to stop their forests, their sacred sites and reindeer calving grounds from being occasionally felled, mined or used for

NATO bombing practice without authorization. At the first sniff of heavy industry and its riches the Samis seem to get shunted fairly unceremoniously to one side.

As if to prove my point, iron ore has been dug out of what is now called Kiruna since the seventeenth century, but in a fairly desultory fashion. It was only when the railway came along in 1903 that the output rose to anything like its current levels and the town expanded vastly. The Kiruna mine produces over 26 million tonnes of iron ore a year, which is exported all over the world – mostly to China. To put that in context, the annual iron-ore output of the US is 47.5 million tonnes, so this single town is producing over half of what the whole of the United States of America can knock out. Impressive. Kiruna's founding father was a man called Hjalmar Lundbohm, an early managing director of the mining company. If you look very hard, you can find the occasional street or civic building or school that isn't named after him. But Lundbohm was evidently a fine man who had some very progressive ideas about communities, health and education, not unlike the great Quaker confectioners back at home.

The Swedes are nothing if not progressive, but it's interesting to note the differences between them and their neighbours just a few miles back in Norway. Having left the train we find a taxi rank, but the taxis that very occasionally come to service it absolutely refuse to pick anyone up. We end up having to ring the number on the back of the departing empty cab to summon the one that eventually arrives for us (in fact the very same cab) some forty-five minutes later. The driver kindly helps us load up the thousand cases, but when we say 'To the Ice Hotel!' (all rather thrilled at the impossible glamour of our destination) we notice he blows into a tube to start up his car. This is extraordinary. I mean, obviously we're used to some engines (outboards, lawnmowers) that you have to pull to start, but a blow-starter? Really? It turns out the car – like many in Sweden – is fitted with an onboard breathalyser, and the driver can only start his car after he has blown into it and been passed 'sober' by the car's computer. It's undoubtedly a progressive idea, but I still somehow prefer a world where you just trust your populace (even at the price of that trust being sometimes broken). I wonder if they'd do that in Norway . . .

But the Ice Hotel! Tee-hee! How exciting. Admittedly I grew up thinking that anything called a hotel was the dizziest height of luxury. Even the shitty place we stayed at in Boulogne once when we went over on the ferry felt to me like something chic and exotic, as if James Bond might suddenly step out from behind the thin plywood door of a neighbouring room. But the Ice Hotel is surely the pinnacle of refined luxury, and yet . . . and yet I can't begin to see how it might possibly work. Surely it can't be like any other luxury hotel. How can you have a bath in your room of ice? How can you possibly traipse about in your Ice Hotel dressing gown, knocking back cheeky half bottles and Pringles from the minibar? How on earth can this work? Well that, I suppose, is all part of the adventure. We pull up at the Jukkäsjarvi Ice Hotel and step out (obviously not until the in-door hand-a-lyser has assessed whether we're wearing gloves or not – this is not true) and gulp it all in.

Wowee, what a heady mix of sublime beauty and exquisite disappointment! It's not one big hotel built of ice at all; it's a huge complex that feels like something between a shopping centre and one of those 'Christmas Wonderlands' that pop up in the Home Counties in the run-up to Christmas each year, whose openings are usually heralded by tales of drunk 'elves' swearing at children and photographs of mudslides taken by 'disgusted' families from the Midlands. The construction of the icy portion of this enterprise, though, which is eventually found at the end of a long snowy thoroughfare lined with shops, is absolutely astonishing and worth travelling all that way to see. Sculptors from all over the world compete to design the individual rooms, and they are all breathtaking. To start with you couldn't devise a more beautiful building material than ice, either in its crystal-clear natural form or reconstituted with snow (to make 'snice', as they like to call it). But then when it's carved and lit from behind (the advent of heatless LED lighting must have been a godsend for this place) it's so sensuously pleasing it makes you want to laugh. The very idea is so wonderfully romantic: every March the ice is cut from the nearby Torne river in what I can only imagine is a faithful re-enactment of the first minute of *Frozen* and is then dragged into cold storage till October, when it becomes the building blocks of this stupendous cathedral of brrrrrr, and then each April/May the rooms and the sculptures slowly melt back into the river. It's gorgeously poetic. Hilariously, as a counterbalance, to comply with EU directives, every 20 yards or so, built into the ice walls, are little alcoves containing fire extinguishers and, yup, there are fire alarm buttons on the walls too. But it adds something to the effect. In the same way that you'd enjoy it if you saw that kind of detail recreated in a doll's house. You just have to forget for a moment that it is actually there through the madness of an unbending law.

This year's ice bar is designed to celebrate the hotel's twenty-fifth anniversary, so you stand in a high-domed room as if in the middle of a splash of champagne, the compacted snice foaming up around you in a perfect likeness of weightless bubbly froth. Cocktails come in glasses made of ice; the designer told me you can get thirteen cocktails' use out of one glass before it melts. If the bar hadn't been stuffed with a considerable proportion of France's *jeunesse dorée* – all in their first beards, jumping up and down and singing Kings of Leon songs loudly amongst themselves – it would have been even more spectacular. But it is truly thrilling to watch the blue refracted light seeping through the ice and feel its firm dry integrity at the constant interior temperature of $-5°$. There are some fairly vapid sculptures here and there outside, but the interiors really are quite, quite beautiful, and there is one sculpture that makes me want to build a frozen wall at home and chat to a local frozen-sculpture freight specialist – it's the huge fern mosaic made of seven-inch-long ice shards embedded into the wall of the chapel.

Chapel? Oh yes, the Ice Hotel has a chapel, because people now come here to get married. I doubt it's consecrated – it doesn't strike me as a religious building as such – it's more that the Ice Hotel, like quite a few places I've come across in my life, has taken on a kind of religious role for travellers, who come here to have profound thoughts, relish being at a focal point of so much fellow feeling, and sing 'Sex On Fire' at the top of their voices in a bar. It's strange that most Western kids, having rejected formal religion, now find themselves inching towards a kind of free-form spirituality, one that takes passages from A. A. Milne as its texts and expresses itself in scented candles and schoolgirl vigils. The Ice Hotel has warmly embraced its role as a temple to this intense but vague questing after truth. On a wall of votive ice plaques in the atrium of the hotel, one reads 'Being happy and healthy and married to Wayne' in what one must hope is a spirit of thanksgiving. I tell you what, if you were to set up a little stall here selling those sky lanterns that people release into the night with candles in, you would make an ab-so-lute killing.

So, yes, the ice architecture of the hotel and the sculpture and design are worth crossing continents to see. Disappointingly, though, the hotel itself is pretty awful. You get your first hint of it as you enter the 1970s swimming-pool-style reception. The strange Catch 22, though, is this: the best parts of the hotel are the ice rooms, but there is literally nothing to do in those except say, alternately, 'Wow' and 'Brrr' and then leave again. The only furniture in each room is a bed (there are no comfy ice La-Z-Boy chairs and ice coffee tables conveniently dotted around), and anyway, even if you wanted to go and hang out sub-zero, the hotel forbids entry to the rooms until after 9 p.m., so you have to kill time in the hotel's permanent structures: either the shops, the restaurant or the beautifully observed student-union-themed cafe/bar. The trick – we are told – is to go to your ice room at the last possible minute; they're for sleeping in only. At this stage I'm still very excited – the sheer novelty of the experience is rather fabulous. I feel like I'm about to go in a flotation tank or walk on hot coals or something and will probably come out saying I will never again sleep above freezing.

The hotel complex is heaving with people: there are about a thousand of them all milling around who have come here not to stay but in large coach parties just to have a look around and in some small way attempt to soak up a vibe. It's not until about eight in the evening that the population thins down to the mere residents. After dinner, you make your way to reception. There you strip down to your thermals and a hat, while locking your clothes in the 1970s swimming-pool-style locker (they've got this theme absolutely licked). They then provide you with an arctic sleeping bag (a colossal, densely feather-packed thing that weighs a ton but which you can feel, even as you drape it around you, will be very good at retaining warmth), a lining and a pair of boots for you to stomp off to your room in. I discover quite quickly that the last person to use my sleeping bag was not entirely up to speed on foot hygiene. The persistent whiff of weapons-grade teensock clings to every fibre and feather of the thing, so on top of the biting cold, the freezing condensation of my breath on the sleeping bag and pillow, the incipient chill gently annexing my bones, the constant dripping of the dew-drops from the end of my nose on to the now icy pillow and the impossibility of finding the light switch to turn off the Northern Lights gobo effect on the ceiling of my room, my every waking breath (oh, I didn't sleep) tastes like I'm head-to-toeing with a particularly devout Hell's Angel.

The crew have had to stay in a concrete chalet with bunk beds and a kitchenette (which is the alternative hotel accommodation on offer), so we're all fairly happy to learn whatever lessons need to be learnt about sub-zero hotels and move on to our next destination. The hotel's extremely nice media-liaison man, Anders (which he absolutely insists must be pronounced 'Andersh' – at a stroke legitimizing our best comedy Dutch/Sean Connery accents), tells us gleefully that the trains back to Narvik are all cancelled due to a storm coming in. Ah yes, this'll be the same storm that kept our car and the camera van from meeting up with us the day before. We're already on Day Two without sponge bags, deodorant, clean socks and pants, etc. We've only been one night at the Ice Hostel (as it has become known) and we're already reduced to smelly grunts with burgeoning beards – you see how easily it happens! Now where's that Kings of Leon album . . .

3

'I Really Hate the Snow': A Kiruna Cabbie Speaks Out

The Swedes we get to know best in Kiruna are the taxi drivers, and them we get to know extremely well, especially now we've got the hang of this ringing-up-to-book business. On the basis of this alone I can tell you that Swedes look like either Fat Jamie Oliver or Fat Nick Clegg (depending whether you get the Volvo estate or the Mercedes minibus) and either of those would be lazy casting for the part of 'Psychopath Red Herring' in a Hollywood serial-killer drama. They all seem to be very good not only at English but also at the witheringly dry aperçu. One gets the impression they've discovered how well this goes down with English-speaking cab-loads, so it may be ladled on a tad. Our taxi out of the Ice Hostel is driven by a Fat Nick Clegg, but the ID card on the dash shows an altogether more 'Paul Gadd' look (bald, goatee, glasses, serial number). We ask how long ago this picture was taken, and he sighs and explains that this is the guy he shares the car with and produces a reassuringly Fat Nick Clegg ID card from the sun-visor flap. Order is restored.

'I really hate the snow,' he notes as we pull out skittishly on to the main road. Then why, we all ask ourselves, do you live high up in the Arctic Circle?

We try the railway station just in case the train info is wrong – certainly the sun is shining and apart from being TITS cold it seems rather clement all in all. But, no, every train has indeed been cancelled; the railway line crosses through some very exposed places at high altitude on the Sweden–Norway border. We turn back to the iron-ore town with the gloomy prospect of another night at the Ice Hotel hanging over us. But oh that we should be so lucky: it turns out the Ice Hotel is full that night (serves us right . . .), as is every other blessed place we try (what is this? Bethlehem?) until one of the older apps on Rog the cameraman's phone tells us there is a Scandic hotel in Kiruna that might be worth a shot . . .

Wahey! There's space! This is suddenly thrilling, as we aren't entirely sure what the alternative would have been. We don't even have a car to sleep in. The Scandic is the upmarket Norse cousin of the Premier Inn, and we've come to love it in every town we've visited so far for its unassuming plainness, stripped-down comforts and liberal attitude to breakfast. 'Where Good Taste Meet' shouts the sexy I-didn't-pay-attention-in-English-class slogan over sumptuous photographs of plates of cod taken with the shallowest depth of field available to the modern camera. There's just time to buy pants and socks and a toothbrush before I get down to the serious business of finding a proper hat, eventually tracking my quarry – like some kind of modern-day Amundsen – to the tourist shop 20 yards from the hotel.

This fox-fur hat will keep me warm for the rest of the trip – we're going to be in temperatures of –35 and below, so I'm not mucking about. You can use various synthetic materials that are OK in moderate temperatures, but for sheer efficiency of body-heat retention (and extreme comfort next to the skin . . .) nothing comes close to the furs and skins of animals. There, I've said it. Reindeer skins are what keep the Ice Hotel from being downright dangerous, as the individual fibres of a reindeer's fur are hollow. Pop a little reindeer skin on a block of ice and it's almost completely insulated – you can sit on it. Then all you have to do is rub a teenager's rancid feet all over it, and boom! There's your bed for the night.

While we're in Kiruna, the storm really begins to whip up – perhaps there was a good reason for cancelling the trains, after all. Bloody hell, it's the first time I've witnessed the ruthlessness of Arctic weather in full sail. To start with there's the wind: easily strong enough to knock you down. Then there's the spindrift, the tiny ice crystals that blow straight into your face – if you haven't got goggles you're done for, as there's no way you can stand in that wind and keep your eyes open or your face uncovered. Someone's hat blows off while we're outside, so a couple of us chase after it, but in no time we're in snow two feet deep and both of us have fallen over. Seriously, getting up in that wind is no joke. It takes me about a minute to get back on to my feet, and if I'd twisted my ankle in the fall I wouldn't have been able to do it. In the space of a *Fortitude* title sequence the snow would've drifted around me, making the whole exercise even more impossible, and by the end of an episode I'd be toast or, rather, whatever the polar opposite of toast is – frozen bread, I guess. Possibly even brown bread. Hilariously, this happens less than 100 yards from the hotel front door and yet is still quite scary. Who'd go out in the wild?

Despite the closure of civilian transport links, there are still iron-ore trains coming through from Narvik (you've got to wonder how bad things would have to get before they'd throw in the towel – maybe the whole place gets ored up if they don't keep the supply chain running, and after two days everyone is just wading around in iron filings, like it's the floor of the barber shop where those magnet guys go to smarten up). The two members of our team who haven't been able to get through to Kiruna (the two with the bags and the cars – the guys who are back in Narvik, gorging on deodorant and high on clean socks) have managed to put a stash of camera supplies (recharging kit, spare batteries, etc.) on to an iron-ore train so we can do something useful while we're there. In the event, the only useful thing we do is pick up the vital supplies the next morning on our way to getting the train back to Narvik. Ah well.

Waiting at Kiruna station for that promised Narvik train is a tedious business, as the train's projected departure time gets pushed back from 10.45 to 11.15 to 11.45 to 12.15 to 12.45. We don't actually leave till 4 p.m., but what an opportunity to watch the hordes of people who come here! For some reason there are loads and loads of Chinese. One of whom – travelling alone, I would guess – strides through the waiting room in army combats with a cold, dead look in his eyes (I mean, obviously everything's cold up here, but the dead look in your eyes shouldn't be weather-dependent) and several hunting knives sticking out from strategically placed sheaths on his rucksack straps. It's interesting to see how quickly the people in the waiting room decide that perhaps they prefer the –15 of the platform after all. I bet he never has trouble finding a seat in a crowded room, although it occurs to me that if he really wants to pull off this dangerous lone-wolf thing he should think of a more 'dangerous lone-sheep's-clothing' approach – just a thought.

When it does finally come, the train is inevitably packed. A couple of English ladies sit down opposite our director and, with the cheerful opening gambit of 'So, what are you filming?', manage to open up a wide-ranging and indeed journey-lasting conversation that takes in everything from their shopping experiences in Sweden, their recent call-back audition for *The Island*, their relationships, their careers, their families, their schooldays, their strengths, their weaknesses, their enduring friendships, what 'makes them tick', all the way through to some jolly anecdotes and a final plea, just before we disembark, for helpful tips on how they can break into reality television.

With the intention of melting unobtrusively into the background, I take the opportunity to bring my diary up to date. After an hour of writing up our time in Kiruna, my attention is caught by a strange sense of something shadowy above me. I look up casually and leap a good four inches into the air when I catch sight of a black-clad teenager looming over my headrest from the seat behind.

'That's good,' he observes generously, carefully reading through everything I've been writing. 'But they take the ice out of the river in March and put it into cold storage. You've got October. It's March.'

In one bound I am on my feet, seizing the collar of his coat in my left hand and twisting it cruelly as I bring his surprised, sparsely bearded face (Fattish Nick Clegg) right up against my nose. 'We consider it bad manners to read other people's stuff without asking first,' I say to him with careful calmness. 'I suggest you mind your own business in future.' Then I lower him back into his seat and return my attention to the laptop and cup of tea before me. Or perhaps I simply mumble vague thanks and turn slightly awkwardly back to amend my information. I can't really remember.

We drive through the night from Narvik station to Tromsø on the worst kind of wet-ice road surface, skidding about like an early departure from *Dancing On Ice*, but, eventually, we end up where Good Taste Meet shortly after midnight. Tromsø, we hear, is 'the Paris of the North' (is there anywhere that isn't the Paris of some compass point or other? And why is it always Paris? What's wrong with, say, Oxford? That's quite beautiful and cultured – fewer titty bars admittedly, but still. I suppose it's just an over-used shorthand for 'an intellectual meeting place that's also easy on the eye', and certainly they seem to have got that right in Tromsø: intellectual meeting place and Good Taste Meeting Place.). 'We'll always have Tromsø' doesn't have quite the same ring about it, though.

Anyway, after the mighty down-tip of snow over the previous twenty-four hours, suddenly everything is back to normal. Norway is back at work and it all seems to be running like a well-oiled Glaswegian hoping to catch last orders. How the hell do they manage this? I suppose the snow isn't something they can claim to be surprised by, like so many British utilities/local authorities/transport hubs. In an attempt at finding out how they do it we decide to chase down the snow-clearing company responsible for Tromsø, and I hitch a ride with Kenove, their ploughman. Neither Fat Jamie Oliver nor Fat Nick Clegg (unsurprising, really: he's Norwegian, not Swedish), Kenove is more Pudgy Matt Damon with a soupçon of Tubby Leonardo DiCaprio thrown in.

The secret to Tromsø's road clearing lies, he explains, in their having three snowploughs so that all round the clock there is at least one on the go. They plough those roads like billy-o till every single one in their bailiwick has a thick mound of snow coiling along beside it, then they come along and blow it up (they even let me have a go at this) through a Fargo-esque chute, sending tons of the stuff shooting high up into the sky to create rather a lovely 'White Christmas' effect about fifty metres downwind. Then, once everything is clear, they send out a grader, which combs the resulting icy surface into ridges so that tyres have got something more satisfying to grip on to. It is extremely slickly and efficiently done.

'Have you ever not been able to go out?' I ask Kenove.

'Nope. We always get out. If a storm comes down and I can't see where I'm going, I'll park up for maybe an hour or two ... there's a bed here' – he waves at the Bower of Supreme Comfort behind me and for a moment I picture Fatt Damon cosying up with his Thermos and a good book while a storm rages outside his cab and suspect this existence probably isn't without its rewards. To start with, the cab is at the top of so many steps – getting into it is like climbing the steps up the side of a gasometer – that you exist on a plane entirely other to that of normal road users. In fact there must be days when Kenove steps down to the roadside only to discover the weather's quite different at ground level.

The following day is the one single date in the whole schedule that I've been dreading. It's the morning of the Ice Swimming. I don't suppose the weather on the day you go Ice Swimming is really all that relevant. Whether it's snowing or bright sunshine makes absolutely no difference to the ice. The ice I'll be swimming amongst. Clink, clink. But for the record it is overcast and a little bit windy.

Because I am going Ice Swimming, I am meeting a club of Tromsø Ice Swimmers. The instructions are extremely simple: I am to meet them at a beach on the far side of the peninsula. Beach? Surely they have another word for the stony bit that leads into the sea when that sea is full of ice because you're about to go Ice Swimming? Come at 1.30! they say heartily, as that's when we'll light the fire! Ah, fire – my friend, I think. I daresay the Ice Swimming Club has a little wooden clubhouse by a jetty and there they'll light the fire so that once we come out of the sauna post-swim, we'll sit by it and drink hot chocolate and eat biscuits . . .

4

Ice Swimming in Tromsø

By the time we've found the right beach, the fire is already lit and it's burning beautifully. There's no clubhouse, as it turns out, just a circle of stones on the beach with this glorious blaze in the middle, and gathered around it are a small group of hearty Tromsø Ice Swimmers, two men and two women, all in late middle age, all in enviably good condition to be honest (is this down to the Ice Swimming?), and all hilarious. 'Welcome!' they shout mirthfully.

I feel like our son Rex looks before he's got an important line in a school assembly: all puffy-faced and grey (he's a pupil not a headmaster). I do quite a lot of laughing rather too loudly. Then, suddenly, all of the things that have stood between me and the Ice Swimming (the morning, the journey here, the walk to the beach, the banter) seem to have disappeared with shocking speed. Gone, all gone, and now the moment is cruelly upon us. The professional Ice Swimmers have all come in their bathers under their Ice Swimming outer clothes (which bear impressive national credentials like 'Norwegian Ice Swimming Team 2012'), so they are all ready in seconds, but I've just brought some bathers in my bag and so have to change right here on the snowy beach.

'What do I stand on while I'm getting ready?' I ask poignantly (does it really matter? I'm going Ice Swimming, after all). Someone takes pity on me and produces a small square of neoprene that is actually a godsend; there is just room to perch on one foot at a time while I hop out of trousers, thermals, socks, etc. Then . . . I'm ready. If I'm going to do this, then 'twere well it were done quickly.

We move heartily towards the waterline like an infantry regiment gathering below the lip of a trench. Strangely, being almost naked in that temperature (−4°) already feels like quite a commitment to the world of cold, so what comes next seems to follow on uninhibitedly. The water is −1. ('Look, minus one!' shouts one of the swimmers, who's dutifully brought his water thermometer with him.) There's nothing for it but to push on and hope to be home by Christmas. I don't think anyone blows a whistle, but it wouldn't be entirely out of place if they did.

With a final instruction to watch out for sea urchins (!) we walk on into the water, adrenaline dulling the searing pain of the icy hit as the gun-metal-grey sea stretches ahead of us. We keep up a decent pace, so ankles, knees, crotch, waist (each of which used to be a milestone when we were little and easing ourselves into cold rivers, lakes or seas) all fall to the enemy advance in quick succession. The next and final cruelty, the moment when the wildebeest falls to the lions, is the shoulders-under moment. It happens in a blur and is followed by several involuntary spasms of frantic swimming (people watching from the beach worry that perhaps I'm going too far out – such is my mania to swim and keep moving) but I am IN.

Apparently six minutes is the longest time anyone has done, though a stout Russian lady they all know who can do twenty does get a respectful mention in dispatches. Apparently you just have to get through the initial three minutes of hyperventilation then the body adjusts, but you don't want to adjust too much because if you stop feeling the cold it's definitely time to get out. The danger point is when the blood leaves the extremities to concentrate on the core: that's when hyperthermia starts to work its magic. I last a little over a minute, after which I feel I can make for the bank without having let myself down.

It's not uncommon, I'm later told, for people to drown as a result of inhaling water while in the early throes of shock. 'Oh really?' I reply, sipping on hot coffee. This whole 'people dying' thing was rather downplayed in the pre-bathe pep talk.

'So why do you do this?' seems a reasonable question to put to the group once we are safely gathered around the fire. 'There must be wonderful health benefits.'

'No,' says the stouter of the two men, the one with what

I now see is an impressively purple nose, 'not really. It's about doing something crazy, because we all need a bit of craziness in our lives.'

It certainly feels good to be alive, standing on that snow-covered beach wrapped in towels and coats and fleeces. There is something faintly exciting (in a hot-curry, endorphin-rush kind of a way) about the pain I've just put myself through. After maybe two or three seconds of utter bafflement, you start to feel the rough jolting friction of so many urgent messages barrelling along so many neural pathways – there's no way this doesn't have a stimulating effect mentally. The only danger is that in your post-swim euphoria you stand about patting yourself on the back for too long with nothing on your feet and wonder why, two hours later, once the sensation has returned to every other part of you, your toes are still numb.

But there's no time to hang around worrying about circulation; we've got to fly further north. Our next destination is Kirkenes, the last town before Murmansk on the Norwegian–Russian border. Kirkenes starts to feel very northern indeed, and it's not just the cold or the lunch-time sunset, it's the street signs: they are all in Russian, which is somewhat ironic as poor Kirkenes was all but destroyed by its Communist neighbours in the Second World War. Only thirteen houses were left standing after heavy bombardment of what had been a massive German base. Now, with the exception of a row of prefab wooden houses donated by Sweden (dubbed 'the Swedish Houses' by some pre-eminent local literalist), most of the town is post-war pebbledash and feels like a Belfast housing estate.

As if sent to brighten our mood by the hand of divine providence, half-Danish, half-Swedish Astrid arrives in her van to take us Northern Lights hunting. She talks very wittily as we head away from the lights of the town, pointing out the landmarks as we go and whipping us into a state of huge anticipation with a lot of Nordic hoopla about what might possibly be the cause of the glorious aurora borealis (spirits dancing, God's displeasure, God's pleasure, spirits angry, God's disco, spirits just mucking about, etc.). She's just moving on from the legends to the science (basically, solar winds around the poles) when we see a faint green glimmer on the horizon. So we pull over and gaze in wonder at it for a bit but then quickly get a bit cold and bored. The stills camera makes it look quite dramatic, but to be honest it's all but invisible to the naked eye. Maybe it only ever looks really good on film – that's the only way 98 per cent of the world's population ever sees it. What if it's all a big photographers' conspiracy and close up it's a bit rubbish? Gulp. I daren't ask Astrid. Even if that were the case I think she's too much of an Arctic true believer (an arctriever) to admit it. She's so keen she turned up for work in just a jumper (well, with some trousers), although she did later put a hat on. It turns out she's based at the Snow Hotel in Kirkenes and is part of the gang of staff there who come back every year for the winter, having been bitten by the Arctic bug.

'It's a temperature thing,' she enthuses (ah yes, hence

the jumper-and-no-coat business). 'You get used to this cold and come to love it. And the light too. Everything looks so beautiful during the polar night. The orangey, bluey, pinky light is spectacular, like a permanent sunset.' I begin to understand the appeal of the light (orangey, bluey, pinky has got to be good, right?), although I do wonder about this cult of 'cold' thing so popular amongst Astrid and her friends. I understand completely about the sociable magic the cold works on people – that was one of the things I had looked forward to witnessing here – but to embrace the cold like this by under-dressing seems fool-hardy, doesn't it? I mean, what would Astrid's mum say if she were here? I haven't met a single person who is actually from the Arctic who makes this great hullaballoo about how they can withstand the cold; they tend to wrap them-selves in as many layers as they need to keep warm. Astrid explains that she and her fellow Snow Hotel people like to go out at night or in storms and just 'experience the cold', whether walking in the snow or 'langlaufing' (like cross-country skiing but more 'German-sounding') through the spindrift. They LOVE the cold. LOVE IT. Simply can't get enough of the stuff. I wonder if this isn't just that time-honoured travellers' thing of wanting to demonstrate how much you belong so people don't mistake you for a tourist. A bit like those students who return from their gap year with an Australian accent or insisting that after four months without shampoo your hair just 'washes itself'.

Astrid drops us off back at our hotel having driven us through a herd of reindeer in the middle of the road, which is rather exciting – at least it is once we've slowed down enough to avoid being in Father Christmas's bad books for the rest of time. At the head of the herd is a beautiful white cow.

'Ah,' cries Astrid, 'that's the Gabba, the famous white reindeer – they're incredibly rare. You maybe see one in your lifetime and it's extraordinarily good luck!'

Well, obviously, I lap that up, as I am feeling pretty lucky – driving through this Arctic night with a tot of whisky in my hip flask, the dimmest Northern Lights on record somewhere vaguely off to my left and a song in my heart. Oh yes, we're blessed all right! Of course it's lucky. I bask in the absorbing glow of sheer good fortune that surrounds us and the good augurs for what is yet to come . . .

What in fact is yet to come is a day of king-crab fishing with Michael, another guide from the Snow Hotel, who drives us out on the very same roads as Astrid did the night before. It's a little bit like a needle going around the same groove of vinyl, though, as Michael seems to have almost exactly the same patter as the rather charming stuff we'd all giggled at with Astrid. It's terribly disappointing to hear her hilarious throwaway gag about the imaginative lake names (they're called First Lake, Second Lake, Third Lake, etc.) and plenty else besides repeated to us verbatim. We all look at each other, slightly hurt, like we've been cheated on. Interestingly, there are one or two subtle discrepancies between Astrid's and Michael's take on things. I mention to Michael that we saw the famous Gabba the night before, expecting him to be thrilled, but his face falls.

'Oh, the Gabba, that's very bad luck,' he warns. 'They're very rare, thankfully, but if you see one it means someone will die.' Happily I don't hold with such ridiculous superstitious claptrap. I mean, really, what kind of idiot would fall for that?

One aspect of Kirkenes life there need be no argument about (except from the odd conscience-stricken vegetarian, but you'll struggle to find one of those in the Arctic – impossible to grow Quorn on the tundra, y'see) is the unrivalled excellence of the king crab as a food source. The Russians' contribution to the well-being of this chilly corner of the world has – as I mentioned earlier – been something of a mixed bag over the decades, but the people of Kirkenes have good cause to thank them for introducing the king crab.

Bloody hell, but they're extraordinary things! It's as if they were designed by a savoury Willy Wonka for ease of catching, preparing, eating and enjoying. They have bred in their millions and millions – possibly even billions – but the Norwegians still apply strict quotas to avoid over-fishing (of course, in American waters off Alaska they have fished the buggers almost to extinction, and this is not the last time in this book that the prudence and restraint of the Scandinavians will leave the more indulgent conspicuous consumption of our Transatlantic brethren looking distinctly second best). King crabs can be up to two metres in whatever the crab version of wingspan is, and despite their spidery appearance they're oddly unthreatening creatures. They have claws, of course, but even these are more vestigial than menacing – nothing like the great Popeye things the ones at home can sometimes wield.

Once we're out on the frozen lake, we are patiently shown how to drill four corners of a hole through about 50–60 cm of ice, cut out a square with a saw and bash the neat Kendal Mint Cake cut-out with an axe so you can have a little Pingu hole to fish through. This scrupulous endeavour turns out to be for demonstration purposes only, as there are several pre-prepped Pingu holes with crab cages far beneath already. So we set about pulling the cages up to the surface and selecting a few of the bigger crabs from our enormous haul.

It's rather a wonderful day out, but because it's been arranged through the Snow Hotel the illusion we've had so far of being Mattin's dogs of war, braving our way through the earth's most forbidding terrain, is slightly tempered. In the interests of health and safety/their amusement, we all have to be dressed up in bright blue padded and fur-lined boiler suits over the top of our (already) many layers and coats, so we waddle about like enormous cobalt grubs on a wedding cake. It doesn't escape my notice that the Snow Hotel guys themselves, like Astrid the night before, barely wear anything – just a jumper and a windcheater. For some reason I find myself getting irritated by this because they're being all cool and Down With The Arctic while we have to grunt about like Weebles, but this must be because I'm either terribly immature or STARVING (most likely both). Luckily help and lunch are at hand.

The crabs are killed as deftly and humanely as possible with a single slice straight down through the shell. We take off their legs and claws, having cut away the gills and other inedible bits, and take them back to the open-air kitchen at the hotel, where we throw them into a huge pan to let them steam for seventeen minutes (this was the magic number for some reason – sixteen's clearly not quite enough and eighteen presumably ridiculously long). I don't think I've ever eaten anything more delicious in my life. Lip-smacking mouthfuls of tight, sweet, succulent white meat – what a lobster might dream of tasting like if it went to the Royal College of Yum and studied really hard. It's like lobster but so much sweeter, it's like crab but so much more satisfying to eat, with a density and texture like monkfish. Even before it's all gone I'm already working out how soon I can have king crab again. Unfortunately they don't seem to serve it at Nando's.

Yet.

5

Polar Bear Training in Svalbard

From Kirkenes we break through to the deep freeze of Svalbard. It's just a shortish flight on a plane, which has to be hosed down by a mechanical de-icing nozzle as we sit on the runway before take-off, but it feels like we're going into another world. Half an hour into the flight the sky darkens – even though it's only 1 p.m. – and a profound coldness starts to seep into the cabin from outside.

This is the deepest into the Arctic we've been so far. From 12 October till 16 February the sun doesn't break above the horizon on Svalbard, and in the depths of December Svalbard is as dark at midday as it is at midnight. Yet by the time we get there it's lit by the most stunning twilight – an Astrid-pleasing palette of blues, oranges and pinks. This is an unexpected treat. It turns out the sun doesn't have to be there for the sky to be beautiful. I didn't quite understand what polar night entails – it certainly sounds rather drear and gloomy not to see the sun for months on end. Turns out to be anything but (as long as you avoid December . . .).

Other aspects of life in Svalbard are markedly less congenial, so it's no surprise to discover that polar bears outnumber humans here. This place is cold, cold, cold. At –23° Celsius your nasal passages freeze when you breathe in. If you're rude enough to spit, it will certainly freeze. And if you wee? Presumably a little arc of yellow ice. But I don't think I'll be trying it; the risks of ending up as one of Mattin's Look-Away-Ladies slides are just too great.

Having determined to keep my extremities safely stowed in their respective compartments, I decide to go for a walk just to experience what life is like at this temperature. Within thirty seconds one plucky soul rides past me on a bicycle with massive thick tyres like a car's, then someone else slides past me on a special walking/sliding scootery thing. It's like the scene in a film where the art department gets to show off all the cool ideas they've come up with for the 'different place' – like the three-breasted hookers in *Total Recall*, or the six-fingered pianist playing Schubert with an added counterpoint (one for the musos there).

My first day on Svalbard is taken up with polar bear training. This is not what it sounds like (at no point does it involve me with a chair and whip trying to coerce some recalcitrant ursine giant to juggle). Polar bear training is mandatory for anyone visiting Svalbard and involves a lesson in rifle shooting, only with a polar bear drawn on the target at the end of the range. In my case it also involves the company of a very tall man called Kim (who has the straggliest, greyest beard I have ever seen) and his wife, Janet (who has no beard of any kind). Kim is a professor from the Norwegian Polar Institute. He has a big yellowish beaky nose that gives him the look of a Jim Henson creation and glasses that make him look like a professor from the Norwegian Polar Institute. Kim takes us up to the Polar Institute's own rifle range where a man called Euden, who speaks English with an accent somewhere between Chinese and Italian, talks us through the protocols of polar bear safety. I ask Kim where Euden comes from and Kim looks nonplussed (a very Kim look) and says 'Norway' (duh!).

Of course Euden's accent when he speaks English wouldn't necessarily tell us anything about where he comes from, just who taught him English. I once met a very aristocratic Russian who'd been taught English by a Liverpudlian and so, for all his rarefied breeding and the smart set he moved in (he was meeting people like me, for heaven's sake!), he was pure Scouse when he opened his gob. Ha!

I ask Kim where he himself comes from originally – no one's from Svalbard, you're not allowed to be born here (no maternity ward at the hospital; expectant mothers are sent away before they're full term) and it's illegal to die here (no undertakers, no registrar, no graveyard or cemetery – if you pop your thermal clogs on Svalbard you are whisked away to the mainland to be registered dead there), so the population is all from elsewhere. Kim looks at me questioningly, as if this is a terribly unreasonable thing to ask.

'I'm from everywhere,' he says (of course he is, with his big yellow nose). He proceeds to rattle off a list of precisely the sorts of places you might expect a little Kim to have grown to manhood (Honolulu, Wyoming, San Jose, Geneva, Stockholm).

'But where,' I try again, 'did you grow up?'

Kim taps his forehead. 'In here.' Then, perhaps seeing the momentary shadow of 'FFS' flicker across my face: 'We spoke Swedish at home, if that answers your question.' I suppose it does, but to tell the honest truth I'm not that bothered, I'm just being polite. Kim's wife Janet looks strangely rattled when I ask her the same question and can't meet my eye when she replies, 'Minnesota'. Maybe there's a rule on Svalbard that you don't ask anyone where they come from, like not asking a bunch of lifers what they're in for. I must try to remember that.

There is something rather sweet about them, though; they talk eagerly with Euden about the wine-tasting dinner he's been at the night before and how they've managed to get tickets to the next one when it comes round in a year's time. It's the chat of ex-pats everywhere. I'm half-expecting the next question to be which part Euden will be playing in *HMS Pinafore*.

Euden does ask me at one point if I've shot with a rifle before, and when I explain that I did when I was briefly in the CCF, Janet turns to me with surprising vehemence.

'No! No! I don't do acronyms,' she insists in that spectacularly forthright way that only academics can get away with.
'You have to tell me what CCF means.' I don't think she's
any the wiser by the time I've explained that it stands for
the Combined Cadet Force, which we did every Thursday
afternoon at school.

Euden's polar bear talk is interesting, not that we'd have
a choice if it wasn't, but it becomes clear – as the talk pro-
gresses – just how likely a polar bear encounter is on
Svalbard, and therefore just how relevant this talk might
be. It turns out that Kim and Janet are here for their
refresher course, as it's been more than three years since
they've been schooled in polar bear essentials. The basic
points Euden drills into us are these: if you leave the settlement for any reason you have to carry a rifle and a flare
gun with you by law, and in the likely event that you meet
a polar bear you have to decide what your particular bear
seems to be up to. If it is loping away and not that excited
by you, then leave it to go about its business, but if it seems
to be stalking you (Euden demonstrates the movement of
the stalking polar bear in a way that suggests he'd be rather
good casting for Ralph Rackstraw should *Pinafore* ever be
on the cards), then fire a couple of flares towards it in the
hope of encouraging it to run off. Nearly everyone I speak
to who has stories of close contact with polar bears –
including Kim – seems to be firmly of the opinion that the
flares are pretty useless and in some cases the flare-round
can even land beyond the bear, so the bang it makes
actually scares it into running towards you, which is

absolutely the, uh, 'polar' opposite of the effect you want to achieve. If this strategy doesn't work, you may need to bring the rifle into play.

The rifle stuff they teach us is pretty much all about safety – loading, making safe and endless demonstrations of how to check your weapon, how to hand your weapon to someone else, how to make your weapon safe, how to double-check that your weapon is safe, how to demonstrate to a blind person that your weapon is safe, etc., etc., etc. However, as with all other courses I've been on up at this latitude, there is an immediate practical element, so nothing is said in vain. It's a sobering fact that on Svalbard all front doors have to remain unlocked so that people fleeing polar bears can run in and take shelter. That's how often people run from polar bears, and presumably how a great many Svalbardian romances start.

Once Euden is satisfied that we are sated with theory, we are ushered out on to the range, where our rifles are all laid out ready for us. Unfortunately, to carry out Euden's crisply relayed orders my gloves have to come off, and it only takes about fifteen seconds of fiddling about with cold metal at –23 before my hands are an agony of numbness and piercing chill. In fact it's a full ten minutes before I can feel them again – hands and feet, that's going to be our main problem here. Wrapping up and keeping your body core warm seems not to be any kind of problem; it's keeping your fingers and toes at a manageable temperature that's the real battle. From today onwards I'm going to wear hot pads in between my layers of socks (I set out with three layers of socks this morning, but from now on it clearly needs to be four).

The light around us that day up on the range is the same celestial lava lamp that we have come to know quite well in the Arctic with its sub-horizon sun, but here it's framed by such an unworldly topography: treeless mountains of so perfect a sedimentary geology that they are table-top flat, powdered and pleasingly drifted with cold, dry snow. I think the way snow behaves with light is instinctively thrilling; whether it's daylight, moonlight, starlight – even Northern Lights light – the snow holds it, spreads it, refracts it in a way that is purest magic. Snow is just beautiful from first to last, from the poetry of its silent falling, the smooth, clean Christmas-cake uniformity of its lying, the fun and anarchy that it introduces to everyday life, and let's not forget the satisfying provision of so much captive water . . .

Just as I'm drifting off into the kind of snowy reverie Kate Bush might make an album out of, I'm brought back to earth with an icy bump. The whiff of competition on the rifle range brings out a new side to Kim. Once he has a loaded gun in his hands, the hippy 'grew-up-in-my-forehead' academic makes a swift exit and there in his place is a dangerously wild mountainman. The straggly beard is no longer the green-tea scented, stroke-me-while-you-read-your-paper-to-the-symposium accoutrement of a thousand senior common rooms; now it's the Jim Beam-soaked whiskers of a maniac. And the nose . . . well, actually, that still just looks like a big yellow nose.

Kim, Janet and I each have different targets but have all been carefully versed in the prone shooting position – lying with one knee out to the side (an unlikely stance to adopt, I'd have thought, in the event of a polar bear charging at you) – as well as the kneeling position and the standing position. Kim is lethal in all three disciplines, managing in most cases to get his rounds so close to each other that they create not two holes but just one slightly enlarged bullet hole. If we were firing arrows, he would be splitting arrow after arrow with each shot. Polar research academic or wanted man? I leave it to you.

Once we've established that polar bears can run at 60 kmh, it becomes clear that deciding to get out your rifle is something you need to do while the poor beast is some way off, probably while he's still deciding whether to be aggressive or not (I'll just play this one by ear – I mean, if he gets his thunderstick out then I'll have him). One thing you see an awful lot of in the Arctic is stuffed polar bears; in fact I'm beginning to suspect it might well be illegal not to have one on prominent display in all public buildings. Each of these monuments of taxidermy is accompanied by a plaque explaining why this particular bear ended up with a rod up its arse and not gambolling out on the pack ice ('This bear was suffering from the trichinella worm and was humanely put down', 'This bear was senselessly mown down by a polar research academic' – that sort of thing).

As we're packing up, Janet asks us who we're making the programme for. 'ITV,' I reply. She does not like an acronym. Glad we've handed the guns back.

6

You've Got (Arctic) Maelstrom

We get back to the hotel. It's worth saying at this point that I get very faint conscience pangs that I'm not Fogling my way around the Arctic, dragging my body weight on a sledge behind me with only James Cracknell's heel blisters for sustenance, as that is almost universally what people imagine to be the set-up for this trip. But, no, there are hotels in the frozen north – each night I am pulling off my twelve layers of clothes in a warm hotel room, FaceTiming my family, listening to Radio 4 on BBC iPlayer and giving myself multiple electric shocks on the brushed steel out of which designers insist on making all hotel lamps.

Another thing I haven't mentioned till now is that I have become a walking Van de Graaff generator up here in the Arctic. I don't know if this is because of all the layers of wool and man-made fibres I'm rubbing together with my every movement or because the Arctic region is especially charged (sounds feasible to my completely non-scientific powers of reasoning), but I am now terrified of anything metallic – even walking in stockinged feet over a brass carpet divider has me leaping like Michael Flatley.

Back at the hotel, then, we hear that there has been a warning from the governor that the biggest storm for YEARS is heading towards Svalbard, likely to hit us the following morning. This sounds very promising. The storm up at Kiruna has whetted my appetite for Arctic maelstroms: boy, are they fun! We try to think of the best place to watch it from, and after a quick call through to the airport manager we get ourselves a date at his control tower for midday, which is just about when the heaviest weather's expected to arrive. I mean, a control tower must be the best place to watch a storm from, mustn't it? This is going to be fun.

One of the many things Kim talked about on our polar bear training was his experience of severe storms and how ill advised it is even to venture outside. 'I find that walking as little as three metres out of our door,' he told us, 'leaves me so completely disoriented by the winds, the noise and the spindrift that I lose all sense of what I'm doing, where I'm going, and which way is up and which way down.'

I am rather excited that they're letting us up into the control tower, particularly at a time of such spicy meteorological goings-on, as these places are normally strictly off-limits. But as we drive off from the hotel, I can't quite muffle the words of Ol' Yellow Nose in my head – might this be the moment we end up getting . . . benighted in the car? The 10-km journey out to the airport is hairy enough – with visibility worsening all the while – but this is clearly nothing compared to how things are going to get.

In the 'air traffic gallery' at the top of the Svalbard airport control tower, a rather taciturn man called Ane is hovering around in a T-shirt. The winds are gathering pace now, and downstairs and all around the thrashing hurricane-force gusts are hurling themselves at anything in their path. Tall security lights on poles bend like ship's masts, eddies the size of canyons spiral above the car park, where our camera vehicle rocks like a teenager's campervan. Inside, however, all is calm. Ane is drinking green tea. The windows are so thick that nearly all sound from the exterior is eliminated, making the scene outside feel like a war film on a muted telly. There isn't actually plainsong chant playing up in that room (I don't think), but for the purposes of my memory let's say there is. The air in there is as warm as a cup of tea that's just reached the point at which you can safely gulp it down, and Ane is so calm and zen that it's hard to be sure exactly how happy he is with his lot, but all flights have been cancelled, so this is basically free swim for him. I'm going to say he's content (which of course is what you want in an air traffic controller), and I could very happily stay in this place all day. With its softly purring computer screens and our 360-degree view of catastrophe, it's hard not to feel like we are actually on the bridge of the storm itself, controlling its awesome destructive powers. Maybe that's what Ane IS doing . . .

Downstairs from air traffic control is the weather station, where Torgei holds dominion. Torgei is a charming man with long hair in a ponytail and a jade symbol tied around his neck on a leather thong. He looks like someone who should have gold discs on his wall in recognition of the many hundreds of thousands of units shifted by his prog-rock outfit back in the early eighties, but, no, Torgei gave it all up for weather and the free electric meteorological department. As various computer models play out the coming tempest for us, the digital consensus seems to be that we are now about two hours from the peak of the storm.

In dramatic contrast with the hermetic environment upstairs, Torgei has a hole in one of his windows through which the wind drones like a wasp in a bottle. This throws our valiant soundman Callum into a state of primal anguish that none of us can raise him from. He tries to block it with everything in his arsenal (mainly radio mic stickies) but to no avail. I suggest that the wind is very much the story here, so we shouldn't worry, but it is a mark of Callum's integrity that any extraneous noise brings him out in hives (and a mark of his professionalism that he doesn't stove my head in with the fluffy end of his boom pole). I remember there used to be a wonderful soundman at the BBC who was colossally posh, had a frantic beard (back in the days when to sport such a thing was really quite a rarity), huge hair and glasses, and was always in Jesus sandals. No day at Broadcasting House or Maida Vale was quite right unless he'd spent at least a quarter of it squirrelling nimbly under desks with his arse in the air surrounded by spills of different coloured cables or pom-pomming among baffling circuitry boards. There's almost an ascetic purism among sound engineers that is a joy to behold. Small film units still tend to be very male dominated, at least in terms of camera and sound operators – I wonder how long that will last – and on those sets the cameraman is apt to be the alpha male, but the soundman is the scholar, i.e. always the one you'd go to for technical help. When my wife rang in a panic one evening because our car had suddenly started doing something weird on the school run, I was sitting next to Callum on the Narvik train and was able to relay precise instructions to her ('Drive in third with the revs between 4,000 and 5,000 for ten minutes and the filters will clear') from him. It cleared up immediately.

Having made it into the heart of the storm (and for heaven's sake it doesn't get more heart-of-storm than this little peninsula of calm protruding up into the chaos), I sit with Torgei and together we watch the weather system on his computer exactly as it closes in on us. I feel like I'm in the lighting box during a Hawkwind gig, and that's not just down to Torgei's jade. This is the first storm I've ever witnessed from 'backstage', and it could be rather a habit-forming experience. Even so, there's a little niggle at the back of my mind that I'm finding harder and harder to ignore. What is it exactly? Ah yes: how the hell are we going to get back to our hotel through this? When Morten the airport manager (thank the Lord! We have finally met someone in Norway called Morten – time was frankly running out) suggests that perhaps we should think about venturing back now before conditions deteriorate even further, I try not to sound too enthusiastic. Morten suggests we travel in convoy, with him going first and Ane bringing up the rear, all with hazard lights flashing. We set off with only three metres of visibility now. It is hell, to be honest. Morten is no more than the length of a car in front of us, but he keeps disappearing. To my left and right the verges will swallow up any tyre that strays on to them, and that will mean an instant benighting (benightenment?) in the car.

At one point I realize I am driving way too fast but, even so, Morten is getting further and further in front of me and is now impossible to see. I feel panic rising within me and put my foot on the brake, only to find I am actually already stationary – it's just the effect of the blizzard swirling around me that's giving the illusion of speed. (I hear the voice of Kim clear its throat in my head.) At this point a tiny gap opens in the icy swirl and I briefly see the blinking lights up ahead again. I seem to have driven off the road, thankfully on to a solid bit of ground, but I have to put on a bit of speed in order to keep Morten in my sights. It's imperative I don't lose him or we're sleeping in the car tonight, but it's also imperative I don't crash into the back of him or . . . well, you get the picture.

After the sort of inch-by-inch journey you might make

in a dream when you're ill, we finally get back to the hotel. It's taken three quarters of an hour of agonizingly slow progress (this morning we made the journey out in under ten minutes). There's not a single landmark visible around us, and it's only by ticking off the various turnings we've made that we know we are back at base. Even in the hotel car park, we could be in the middle of the wilds for all we know – the building is only 30 feet away but there's not an inkling of it. What Kim had said about losing all sense of time and place in the middle of a storm was spot on.

The following day, when the weather clears, it is hard to conjure up the genuine fear and panic we'd all felt driving back the night before. Perhaps it had all been a terrible over-reaction; what, after all, was the worst that could have happened? Well, self-evidently, we would all have been fine. But however much of an illusion the danger might have been, the fury of the storm as it screamed around us, and the lack of certainty in the moment that it would pass at all (what if it didn't? What if it raged on for days . . . ?) made it a much more difficult situation to handle rationally. Rather like being shut in a box or trapped in a lift: that mental equilibrium you could normally rely on to tell you everything will be fine is the first thing to disappear. That said, I noticed Morten and Ane both seemed remarkably unfazed. Norwegians, y'see?

The following day is 16 February, which – had this most auspicious of new mornings not been heavily overcast – would technically have offered us the first glimpse of sun in Svalbard since 12 October. A tiny sliver of the fiery ball had been due to appear over the hilly horizon like a Chad over a wall (remember Chads?!). We've been planning to travel over the glacier to watch this important seasonal rite of passage and salute the shiny orb, but as it's happening behind the cloud there seems little point, so we decide instead to head off on skidoos (this is huge fun – an activity that somehow seems rugged and outdoorsy despite requiring no more effort on the part of the rider than simply to sit fatly on a very comfortable padded seat and rev the throttle) to an old trapper's base. The prospect of encountering a bit of Svalbard's pre-industrial heritage is obviously an exciting one, but beyond that we are hoping to meet up with an Englishman called Alexander Pilditch, who I'm hoping will be able to give us the inside track on life in Longyearbyen. He's been living here for four years, ever since arriving as a student. Longyearbyen, the main settlement on the Svalbard island group (an archipelago known once upon a time – and to this day by people who want to let you know that they're serious Arctic types – as Spitsbergen), has a university (hence Pilditch enrolling here), a population of 2,040 and a roaring trade in taxidermy. The other settlements on Svalbard are Barentsburg, a barely populated Russian mining settlement, and Ny-Ålesund, which is really just a research station and a shop (early closing Thursdays).

Alexander works for the satellite control centre on the island. I remember nodding a lot at the answer he gives when I ask him what he does there, but in truth quite a sizeable portion of what follows flies (much like the satellites themselves) over my head. It seems there are countless satellites that are 'polar orbiting' (which I take to mean they fly directly over the North and South Poles), so on Svalbard and somewhere correspondingly southern in the Antarctic there are huge monitoring facilities. I find it rather thrilling to think of all that vital technical data which is then disseminated all over the world being initially gathered by people like Pilditch in the two most barren outposts on the planet. It's like being told that iTunes is run from a small bothy in the Cairngorms. Pilditch then says something about satellites crossing above Svalbard fourteen times a day, which I think doesn't sound too arduous – only fourteen satellites a day to monitor? No, he explains, each satellite orbits the earth fourteen times a day. That's quite fast. 'Yes,' says Alexander Pilditch, 'they travel at five miles a second.' Somewhere in my brain there's a faint pop.

Before hearing the siren call of the satellite monitoring business, Pilditch was in the Territorial Army in the Officer Training Corps (or in the OTC of the TA, if Janet's not around . . .). This becomes immediately evident on speaking to him; he has got the art of 'talking Army' absolutely curled up and purring like a kitten in his hand ('When you've taken your coats off, we're going to go over there to get you kitted out with boots, mittens and oversuits. OK? Right, let's all go over there to get you kitted out with boots, mittens and oversuits . . .', 'Obviously the last thing I want to do is to be firing at a polar bear, but if I am attacked by one then I am afraid there is going to be one dead bear . . .', 'Now, if you're looking at those reindeer and wondering to yourselves what they might be doing over there by those houses, then the answer is "feeling pretty bloody miserable, I should think"').

Alexander professes himself very happy to be single because, he points out, this means he can spend his money on the kind of rifles normally only the military get to shoot and he doesn't have to worry about 'buying chocolates' instead. I suspect the kinds of girls he might date in Svalbard would go crazy about his gun – they'd get a whole lot of Pilditch and extra polar bear protection thrown in for free – but Pilditch is having none of it. I suddenly have a flash-back – I've seen Pilditch before! Yes, he was the man on the thick-tyred bicycle when I ventured out on my first night. It's beginning to feel like a play where cast members are doubling up and 'Man On Bike' from the opening scene and Alexander Pilditch from the second act are being played by the same person . . . He tells me that his Longyearbyen existence has become so ingrained now that when he goes home to his parents in Malvern he finds himself instinctively going to fetch his rifle before taking the dogs out for a walk, then presumably slapping himself on the forehead with the heel of his hand when he remembers he isn't in Svalbard. I can see how the constant rifle drill up here might seep in and become second nature, just because the day you forget your rifle could easily be your last. All I'm saying is if I were a neighbour of Mr and Mrs Pilditch Senior back in Malvern and owned a large white dog I'd be very nervous.

The bizarre landscape, with its strict sedimentary rock and flat-top cliffs, gives the valleys we pass through a somewhat lunar quality, and the light on this first day of 'sun' above the horizon is awesome despite the cloud cover. Strangely, we find we lose all sense of distance. Cliffs rise up ahead that you'd swear were no more than half a mile away, only to find that half an hour later you are still speeding towards them at 40mph.

Alexander Pilditch has a rather debonair side-saddle technique of riding a skidoo, which involves standing on one leg and kneeling on the seat with the other. This has the advantage of allowing you to start your skidoo while walking alongside it so you can then hop across with a jaunty little manoeuvre on to the running board. And this has the advantage of being something no one unschooled in the Way of the Skidoo would be allowed to attempt and therefore marks out the adept from the mere holiday skidoo-driver. I remember, aged about eight, telling my friend Tommy Dower that he would never know as much about kagouls as I did, because I'd had one for a year and he'd only just got his first kagoul, I wonder if I recognize in Pilditch's little skidoo jig something of the same sentiment.

The old trapper's house, when we get to it after a couple of hours of ACE skidoo-ing, is a tiny three-room hovel on the edge of a fjord that has completely frozen over. We have left the bleak outpost of Longyearbyen miles and miles behind us, and it is an unbelievably magical spot. As we sit and look out at the bay, the thick ice rises and falls like a sleeper's stomach – croaking and groaning and displaying all the signs of being a living thing.

I grew up in Northumberland (I may possibly have mentioned that), quite a long way from the middle of nowhere (we were more on the edge of it). Our nearest village (Rothbury) was almost five miles away, although Pauperhaugh, a mile away at the bottom of the hill, was nominally a village, despite having only a farm, a post office and a telephone box to its name (imagine that now, getting a post office when there's only six people in the village, including the postmistress herself!). This means that I am predisposed to remote areas, I guess, but curiously I have only ever felt remote and lonely under a lowering sky. In Northumberland, when the sky was clear and the sun shone, it felt like we were near the centre of the universe, right next to where the thrum of life was emanating from. The minute the weather closed in (as it does often, especially with the sea fret coming in from the coast) I felt like we lived as far from human habitation as it's possible to imagine.

The light of Svalbard, the unique quality of the colours in the sky that make each day feel like one long golden hour (by which I mean that summery evening time when photographers like to get snapping to capture the best of the light, rather than Simon Bates playing hits from yesteryear) and the huge horizons on all sides make this trapper's cottage with its cosy fireplace and kitchen table feel like somewhere I could happily settle down to spend some time. The trapper lived here with his wife for decades in perfect self-sufficiency. Obviously my wife would take some persuading (and I'd want to be able to get Radio 3, oh and an Ocado delivery at least once a week), but I reckon I'd be blissfully happy.

I've often wondered where I would live if for some reason I didn't live in England. It's rather a fun exercise dreaming of a life in the Dordogne, or in Paarl or Franschhoek in the Cape Winelands, or what about relocating to Oregon or Maine or the Shetland Islands? None of these are impossible to contemplate, but I would move to Norway in a heartbeat. In the short time I've been in this magnificent country I have fallen head over heels in love with it. The countryside itself is so heartbreakingly beautiful, like an exotic and more louchely brought-up cousin of the landscape I grew up in. The climate, evidently, is not hot – although that has its season too – but it is the most conducive to happiness I have ever come across. Best of all, though, are the people. Geography and weather, social customs and trends of migration all conspire to shape the characteristics of a country. Of course it's ridiculous to talk about an entire race having such-and-such a personality, and just because I'm complimenting them rather than damning them doesn't make it any less stupid, but even so . . . I have come across such humanity and decency in Norway, such intelligence, such advanced social ideas (I haven't even touched on their revolutionary penal system, which has all but eliminated reoffending!), such entrenched contentedness and warmth. It turns out it's not an act at all, they're just wonderful, wonderful people.

* * *

We sit in the departure lounge at Svalbard surrounded by all our new friends. Why, who's that over there behind the newspaper? What? With the frenetic chin hair and yellow nose? Sure you know who that is – it's old Kim from the firing range! Ah yes . . . and that man skulking by the cold-drinks fridge, he looks familiar too. Don't tell me you've forgotten Ane, the rather intense gentleman from the air traffic control office in the tower? No, of course I haven't, it's just . . . it's just . . . What is it, man? What's eating you? It's just ... if he's down here ... (Yes, come on, out with it!) ... then WHO'S CONTROLLING THE AIR TRAFFIC?

As it happens, it's Ane's week off from the control tower (PHEW), so he is flying back home to Lofoten for a week: 'I always try and go back for the skrei,' he says, neatly and unwittingly tying up our Norway story into a perfect round bundle. In all our time there we get no better illustration of Svalbard's (and in a way Norway's) tiny-ness and sweetness than this final glimpse. I'm expecting at least one of our fellow passengers to be stopped at the gate: 'But, Aesgeir, you can't go. What if my root canal needs treating and . . . hang on! Who the hell's going to run the department of agriculture while you're away? And I suppose this means "Tums 'n' Bums" class won't be happening on Tuesday . . . Shall I tell Bodil or will you?'

Part Two

Explorers' Graveyards: Iceland, Greenland and the Northwest Passage

7

Reykjavik: Home of the Six-Gait Pony

Here's something strange that I've never mentioned to anybody before. Occasionally I hear the late Queen Mother's voice in lifts. There we are, my secret's out. This isn't some strange mental thing, I hasten to add – Lord, at least I hope it isn't – I'm pretty sure it's a voice inside the lift rather than a voice inside my head. Pretty sure.

There used to be some rehearsal rooms in an old Victorian building on Shaftesbury Avenue, some kind of church hall I seem to remember. It was one of those places with huge, cold stone staircases that smell of the huge, cold stone loos that nestle in the dusty turnings on every floor. The place has long since been demolished, of course, to make way for clean glass, concrete and steel – almost certainly a step in the right direction in terms of general modernity, but hell, I'll miss those old civic buildings once they've all been turned into shiny Renzo Piano Meccano. Apart from anything else, where will all the actors go to speak to each other in comedy Scottish accents and pretend to do the *Guardian* crossword whilst waiting for auditions, for heaven's sake? Heartbreaking, really. Anyway, where was I? Oh yes! That church hall was the first building whose lift I distinctly remember being voiced by HRH the Queen Mother, Gor Bless 'Er. And I'm absolutely certain it was her.

'Doors Closing,' it used to say in a regal voice with just a mischievous hint of Dubonnet in its careful cadence. 'Third Floor,' it would then add with an adamant neutrality of inflection, as if to say, 'I honestly have no idea if you'll get the part.'

I would like to get to the bottom of this mystery one day. Was it really the Queen Mother? Did she at some point (like the Prince of Wales dutifully pulling a pint in a pub – evermore to be shown in a faded photograph, squinted at by sozzled lunchtime regulars behind the pickled eggs) sit behind a Popper Stopper mic guard, surrounded by smiling men in heavy mayoral gold links and generous frostings of shoulder scurf? And did she, after a few carefully chosen words for level, lay down some lift verbals? ('Sorry, Ma'am, love, you're popping a bit on "doors" – can we have another?')

Anyway, what I am teeing up here is the glorious discovery that the hotel we are staying at in Reykjavik also has a Queen Mother-voiced lift. And for heaven's sake, why not? If not here, then where? Cometh the hour, cometh the lift. It seems perfectly of-a-piece with this mad place of hot and cold, this misty mountained land of Vikings. I slept for much of the flight here, quite deeply, and spent the journey into Reykjavik from the airport staring at a flat black landscape of lava (obviously dried lava or whatever you might call it – cold lava, set lava – not the wet stuff, which I understand can be quite warm), and as far as the eye could see (which needless to say was FAR!) there wasn't a soul, nor a dwelling, nor an animal.

There is the odd moment in life when you wonder if you mightn't have actually died and not so much gone to heaven but gone somewhere like this – an astringent Valhalla of sibilant winds and low black horizons. And in such a place you shouldn't be that surprised if one of the first voices you hear is the disembodied one of the much-loved late mother of our monarch telling you whether you're going up or down.

Reykjavik itself is a curious sight – famous to all who grew up in the eighties for the Reagan–Gorbachev summit that took place here in 1986 (only two years after Reagan and Chernenko lookalikes had been knocking seven bells out of each other in Frankie Goes To Hollywood's 'Two Tribes' video). It's not greatly beautiful – although we later discover a very pleasing little enclave of restaurants and bookshops (lots of bookshops and what appears to be a library – an admirable amount of reading goin' daan in Reykjavik, unless it's just a pick-up joint for the better kind of young Icelander) in a network of narrow streets that must be the old town. But a lot of Reykjavik is made up of buff-coloured tower blocks of drab shape, and pebble-dashed terraced housing (Shankill Road once again swims to the front of the mind – we even find murals at one point, although not so much of balaclava-clad Orangemen as of, well . . . a faintly erotic close-up of lipstick application and someone who looked very much like former chancellor Norman Lamont, although obviously it can't have been him – it must just have been someone's granny).

Norway poses for photographs from the minute you arrive. There aren't many vistas that don't pout at you until you stop and click away – it even lays on nice lighting too. The tiny little bit of Iceland we've seen so far doesn't seem to do this so much, or at least not in February (I'm not blaming it, I'm merely noting a different modus operandi); it goes more for the dramatic. This is after all a land that has grown up out of a crack in the earth's crust – a blistering spillage, essentially – and such a dramatic evolution can't help but lend the landscape a theatrical quality. Where the Ice Hotel was – rather beautifully – a stolen, frozen moment that then melted back away into the river, Iceland's landscape has a kind of elemental violence and power frozen not in ice but in stone.

Iceland certainly answers a lot of questions for me – all right, not the one about HRH the Queen Mother and the lifts but certainly about the Northumbrian landscape I grew up in. The huge slabs of surface stone with their twinkly quartz, the peculiar springy, ash-y quality of the soil in places and of course the lichen and heather that grow so happily in that soil and on that rock – I now know, thanks to Iceland, that this is volcanic pure and simple. Where Northumberland has verdant valleys and then large areas of craggy uplands and moorland, the Icelandic landscape seems to be craggy uplands and moorland and then large areas of bare jagged rock. The agriculture, such as it is, appears to be entirely hill farming (upland grazing for sheep and horses – apparently there are cattle too, although I haven't seen any yet) and fodder crops.

In Norway and Sweden they are aware of – and celebrate – their Viking past but it seems to survive more as a sort of colourful historic sideshow like morris dancing or playing the sackbut. It's something they put on in the form of Viking 'attractions', whose pamphlets fill up hotel front desks. Iceland's Viking heritage, on the other hand, is a chapter that hasn't closed – they still are Vikings – it's all around you all the time, preserved whole like a mammoth in the ice. It is an absolutely unbroken, adamantine bond with the past, and its culture is proudly held up as the origin of all Icelandic life, its politics, even its religion. Until fifteen years ago, when outsiders started coming here to live and work, every single person on the island knew exactly what their Viking origins were, which branch of which clan they belonged to. They still do, of course; it's just there are some people on the island for whom that's a very short game.

Being an island nation, and a culture of inveterate storytellers and event recorders, they know every detail of every family back to the day the nation's founding fathers decided it wasn't a terrible idea to stay here. There is a famous book, the Íslendingabók, which points the careful user towards his or her lineage. It's now an app, so that you merely need to feed in your social security number to be given chapter and verse on your forebears.

Better still, if you feed in two numbers it will tell you how they're related. I did ask if that was handy for checking that your potential date wasn't a second cousin, and the girl looked at me like I was mad (or a close relation) and said, 'Yes, of course that's what it's for.' (The 'duh!' was unspoken, but it was definitely in there somewhere.) I thought I was being hilarious. The Norse culture is protected pretty robustly, but if you are an outsider you are quickly brought into the fold. I discover, for example, that when you name a child you have to get approval from a naming committee for the names you have chosen. If the name is a foreign one, then it will be put into a Norse idiom and spelling. This explains why I haven't yet met a single Chardonnay or Courvoisier in Iceland . . .

It's not just the people who are still Vikings – every species on the island seems to have some sort of Viking pedigree. Certainly the horses do. These are peculiar to Iceland (in the hope of preserving their uniqueness, it's illegal to bring any other kind of horse into the country – and fortunately horses are just about big enough not to arrive hidden in a bunch of bananas) and have been bred (or rather NOT bred) to be the horsey answer to the Manx cat. (I mean, they have a tail and everything, they're just a bit smaller than normal horses and, well, they're Viking, aren't they?) Apparently these horses have two additional gaits. I know, I had no idea either, but I gather it means they have six gears: Walk, Trot, Something unintelligible with lots of øs and ∂s, Canter, More øs and ∂s, and Gallop.

Apparently there are also Viking sheep. I can't think what their particular qualities might be so let's just say they are bred to make those hairy Icelandic jumpers and for ease of counting for Norse insomniacs.

While some questions may remain as to the exact parameters of the Viking farm-animal subset, the harsh realities of Glima wrestling – the ancient Viking art form of throwing someone on to the floor in a forceful but comical way – are all too apparent to me. At least they become so in the course of the brutally effective demonstration of its destructive potential for which I am used as a guinea pig/stooge by a lovely girl called Eva, who narrowly missed out on being the Glima Queen in April 2014. (She competes again this year; in fact as you're reading this she may well already be the holder of the coveted Glima necklace. I hope so – GO, EVA!!)

We pull up at a gym and I am led inside, at this stage quite unaware of what – other than wrestling – is in store. I am kept in blissful ignorance and a small locker room surrounded by murals of Vikings with long hair and umlauts while the crew get everything ready. I have been told that I am meeting a champion wrestler (the gender of whom has been kept secret). Several enormous gym members come and go and nod in a friendly manner. If they're wondering what this strange person's doing sitting idly in their changing room, they're nice enough not to say anything. Finally I am called up to meet my opponent on the gym floor. Not, as it turns out, some hulking troll with a beard and a protruding forehead but a very giggly nineteen-year-old girl. Phew!

By the time Eva has finished levelling the concrete with me, my grasp of the whole Glima procedure is somewhat shaky amid the beginnings of a mild concussion, but the memories that come to me in the night involve wearing a complicated strap arrangement around your crotch that looks like the leather skeleton of a pair of pants (if pants had leather bones, you understand? Is this making any sense?). Your opponent grips you tightly by two bits of your strap – one on the upper west side and one on the lower east – and you return the compliment. Then begins a curious tango where the two combatants stride – probably rather gracefully when done by Eva and her Glima rivals but not so much when it's me – from leg to leg in a deceptively friendly kind of a way.

The whole ballroom feel of the encounter is further enhanced by the generous trouser flare and tight, shimmering manmade fabrics we both seem to be wearing (rather tighter than comfortable in my case, thanks to ex-Major in the Marines Paul Mattin's carb instructions – God, he's going to cry into his rations when he learns that we didn't spend fifteen hours a day yomping across the ice caps, smothered in improvised camouflage cream). Then suddenly, with no warning at all, a leg is stuck out by my opponent, my straps are pulled up and, with a bone-jarring whump, I'm lying on the floor in a daze.

I ask Eva through a circle of bells and cuckoos if we might perhaps go back to the rudiments of Glima so she can teach me the basic tenets. This is the only way I can think of to distract her from hurling me to the floor repeatedly. 'Ah yes, of course,' says Eva. 'Let's do that.' Phew. Eva stops hurling me to the floor repeatedly. But only so she can now demonstrate the Eight Throws of Glima on me one after the other, which amounts to almost exactly the same thing. She lulls me with her waltz steps in much the same way as an osteopath hugs and rocks you before wrenching your very being into a new and unexpected future. Whump! Whump! Whump! Whump! Down I go and down again with the slap that only 84 kilos of point-less flesh can make on a meagre strip of thin rubberized bunge about the thickness of a curry-house menu, spread thinly over solid concrete.

This isn't entirely what I had been hoping for when I asked about 'the rudiments'. After about my fifth bounce, I start to put up a bit of resistance to Eva's effortless throws. I am developing the kind of headache that hangs out at the top of your spine, not really assigned to any particular zone, just happy to help out where it's needed: a supply headache, if you will. But the moment Eva senses resistance on one side, she swings her other leg around and flings me on to an altogether different bit of floor. Whump! Whump!

Whump! On and on it goes as the nearly once and future Glima Queen seeks to make me one with the floor of a Reykjavik gym – and not even really with the air of a fighter either; it's all performed with the languid air of a laundress ironing a hanky.

After twenty minutes or so, which I notice the crew have enjoyed immensely, Dom our director seems to think he's got enough footage of me flying through the air upside down. Eva, needless to say, has hardly broken a sweat; she could evidently keep doing this all day, but I am rather thrilled when the bout is brought to an end. We chat briefly about the various championships Eva's got coming up and what the chances are of her winning the title this year (VERY high, I reckon!) and before long I am gratefully back in the locker room peeling off the spandex.

If the gym you go to happens to be in the far north, I suppose you'd develop some special trick for stepping out into the extreme cold. I find I'm usually roasting hot for about half an hour after a workout, but here I've got to climb into all my endless layers of thermals while still in my post-gym fug. I reckon the seasoned Arctic gym bunny (they're the ones with the silver markings) keeps several layers in a rucksack so that they can be applied as they walk down the street. My Viking chums on the walls with their umlauts are giving nothing away. I notice they're mainly wearing leather straps and helmets, which strikes me as a recipe for pneumonia on one hand but rather a good album cover on the other.

Although my many die-hard Death Metal chums assure

me that Norway and Sweden are the heartland of that much misunderstood musical genre, the whole Viking/Heavy Metal crossover is much more noticeable in Iceland than it was in Norway. Viking script and Heavy Metal fonts are kind of one and the same, and the whole Glima get-up is so unbelievably Derek Smalls that I begin to suspect the seeds of Heavy Metal might have actually come over in the longboats. I'd always assumed Vikings and Metallers just shared a convenient liking for long hair and abhorrence of soap, but I wonder for the first time if the cultural resonances mightn't go deeper than that. The whole thing comes to a wart-encrusted head in the Viking midwinter festival of Thorrablot (midwinter coming in late February, of course, as the season in Iceland goes on for bloomin' ever).

Sadly we will have left for Greenland before the festival starts, so I never get to see the Thorrablot in its pomp, but just being in Reykjavik for the build-up gives us more than enough of a 'flavour'; in fact one that will linger on for days. One of this demanding event's many culinary highlights is a dish of sour ram's testicles (sourness seems to be very important, as it features again and again across the festival sweetmeats). Among the numerous enticing ales specially brewed for the festival, the one that has got everyone talking is the dung-smoked sour ram's testicle-flavoured beer . . . There we go, more testes. Not for the first time I wonder if this Viking business doesn't get a bit 'stag weekend' at times. I ask if the testes are a fertility thing, but the look I am given implies that, no, it's just a testicle thing. The beer does have a sour note to it (absolutely crucial) and, yes, if you keep chewing it over you can just make out the smoke. Thankfully the dung and testicle elements are polite enough to hide behind the more essentially beer-y tangs.

For this illicit glimpse of the Thorrablot bill of fare I am indebted to Kevin, a jovial Irishman with an impressive ginger beard who runs a bar some way out of Reykjavik. I suppose when your country of origin differs from your country of domicile by only one letter you must feel some sort of extra obligation to make the difference clear to casual observers. I notice that Kevin does this in a very subtle way, allowing just a tiny hint of his Irishness to percolate through so that only the most discerning listener can pick up on it. I ask him what had brought him up here to the cold.

'Ach-to-be-sure-twas-as-an-archaeologist-that-I-forst-came-here-that-is-to-say-I-came-to-do-a-study-of-the-inland-waters-I'm-a-marine-archaeologist-to-be-sure[wink]and-ye-know-ach-something-about-this-place-got-to-me[breath]I-fell-in-love-with-yer-archetypal-Icelandic-girl[wink]ach-once-I'd-seen-beauty-like-that-to-be-sure-I-was-never-going-to-leave [wink, breath] I-know-what-you're-thinking-you're-thinking-why-did-she-fall-for-him-because-you'll-have-noticed-I-have-a-face-for-radio-ha-ha-ha-ha [wink, breath] ach-well-I'll-tell-you-plain-to-be-sure-it's-because-d-men-up-here-yer-heroic-Iceland-types-they-don't-have-any-social-skills [breath] sure-they'd-disappear-rather-than-talk-to-anyone [wink,

breath] so-if-you-meet-an-Icelandic-beauty-and-you're-
outgoing-and-have-a-sense-of-humour-like-ach-then-it-
doesn't-matter-if-your-rival's-a-Nordic-Adonis[wink]to-
be-sure-you-go-to-the-front-of-the-queue-I'm-now-a-
married-daddy-of-one-ach-to-be-sure.'

At this point Kevin takes a thoughtful puff on his little
pipe and removes his enormous green hat. Or possibly
not. Anyway, whatever else one might say about Kevin –
and he's certainly got a few things to say himself – you
can't deny he's outgoing. Iceland's gain was Ireland's loss
in that regard. In his other professional capacity Kevin is a
dive guide, and so he is taking me to 'snorkel the Silver
Lady', which from Kevin's mouth could mean literally anything, but actually means something reassuringly similar
to how it sounds.

The west of Iceland clings to the edge of the North
American tectonic plate, the east to the Eurasian, and
down the middle runs a rift that when it disappears under
the sea turns into the Mid-Atlantic Ridge, the longest
mountain range on the planet (albeit one that exists almost
totally underwater). The Silfra – or Silver Lady (I never got
to the root of how that, of all the possible names, should
be the one that stuck; perhaps David Soul came here once)
– is the fissure between the two tectonic plates, the result
of which is a very large gully, along which Kevin and I are
going to snorkel.

We do so on a sunless, snowy morning, having driven
out from Reykjavik in the dark to a bare patch of moorland about forty minutes away. We change into our

snorkelling things in a little empty car park and waddle along in our flippers to the head of the ridge. Once there we stand at the top of a kind of fire-escape stairway that leads down into the dark waters of a narrow stream. We are in the remotest, bleakest landscape imaginable. On one side of the ridge (the North American) it is absolutely treeless. On the other (the . . . well done: the Eurasian) it's dotted about with conifers and dwarf birches (they never really seem to make it beyond shrubhood, summer's lease hath all too short an etc., I suppose) and the level of the land on this side is about 10 metres lower ('due-to-tectonic-movement-to-be-sure-and-ach-weren't-we-always-pulled-down-by-the-Americans [wink]').

What we're perching on the edge of looks for all the world like a burn in a Highland bog: an unassuming little 10-foot wide stream that appears from underground and runs a wavering course for 500 yards or so before throwing in its lot with a lake. It's the sort of stream you might be tempted to cast a salmon fly on to in better weather. The edges of the burn hang heavy with snow, there are little islands here and there, stacked with snow and ice, and above it Kevin and I are tightening our fins and doing a bit of mental preparation for the hit of cold. ('Ach-it's-better-than-Botox-to-be-sure-you'll-have-lips-Angelina-Jo-lee-would-give-her-eye-teeth-for [wink] and-ach-sure-you'll-see-your-wedding-tackle-again[breath]probably-sometime-next-mont' [wink].')

I am in a dry suit − a new experience for me − which allows me to wear a cosy thermal onesie underneath but still leaves hands and feet rather exposed. The feet are in rubber slippers that are part of the suit, and the hands have neoprene mittens, but looking down at the grey water and its snowy verges I'd prefer a woollier, more solid encasement, something altogether more like a house with a roaring fire in it. At least the water isn't freezing, I opine, noting the absence of ice layers. ('Ach-that's-just-because-it's-flowing-too-fast-to-form-ice-just-remember-to-be-sure-however-cold-it-gets-no-weeing-in-d-suit.')

We plunge in. The dry suit is miraculous: I've been bracing myself for the Bugger-Me cold of the Ice Swimming, but, no, it is beautifully un-life-threatening. The other boon of the dry suit is its buoyancy, which means that with the insistent current leading down the gully you don't especially need to do anything at all except stare down towards the bottom of the fissure, clasping your hands behind your back like the Duke of Edinburgh at some underwater civic event. Anyone who's snorkelled doesn't need me to wang on about the magic of the sub-aqua landscape, but, even taking that as wanged on, this is something else.

The first thing to strike me – after I've adjusted to the eerie silence from Kevin – is the visibility. You can see absolutely gin-clear water for 150 metres at least. This is glacial water, which is apparently milky when it leaves the glacier, but by the time it's worked its way (for some improbable, millennial period) through the porous volcanic rock, it is so unbelievably clean that Kevin and I are the only impurities in the whole waterway. If a sudden thirst comes over me during the expedition I can just spit out the mouthpiece and drink my fill of purest mineral water. That's quite a fun thought. I probably won't be doing it – who knows where Kevin's been – but it feels decadent to be swimming in such purity.

I remember my cousin Daisy, who was once a diving instructor, explaining to an uncle that views underwater could often be just as beautiful – if not more so – than those above water. Uncle Harry took one look at her down his nose and said, 'What rubbish', and the subject was closed for ever. It turns out this modest little bog stream reaches down to cavernous depths of 40–45 metres, and in such crystalline conditions that the light travels right down to the lava rock at the very bottom, which shines bright red against the subtle cool aqueous blue. In places the rocks on either side form sheer walls; there's one long stretch known, for pleasingly obvious reasons, as The Cathedral (not, as far as I'm aware, a David Soul reference), and there you get the weird sense that you might be looking up into a clerestory rather than down into a boggy stream.

Every so often I have to tear my gaze from the beauteous deep to look above the water, just to remind myself of the sow's ear from which this purse is woven: nothing but a humdrum moorland stream edge with a whippy wind stirring up rivulets and kicking a drift across the surface of the water and into my face. But the contrast is what this natural wonder is all about. Imagine walking for twelve hours into the middle of the Yorkshire Moors and stumbling across a natural amphitheatre in which a full-scale production of *Tristan und Isolde* is just reaching its Act 3 climax and you'll get some idea of how bizarre this experience is. Interestingly, as I look above and below the surface of the water, I can see a swirling mist just below the water line, this ('ach-to-be-sure') is what water looks like when it's below freezing and trying to coalesce into ice. The current at this point is having none of it, however, and the formation of ice clearly isn't going to happen until much later, once the fast-moving water of the gully has settled down in the lake.

Eventually Kevin and I haul ourselves out and run (more to magic up a bit of heat, to be honest, than in the interests of speed) along the moorland path back to the car park and our warm clothes. In the ninety minutes we've been gone this desolate spot has turned into a fairground of minibuses and big-tyred 4x4s ('Ach-I-don't-suppose-they're-making-any-kind-o-statement-about-their-manhoods-wit-those [wink]'), all of which are spilling out crowds of snorkellers and snapping tourists. It's extraordinary that Iceland's very remotest areas are becoming famous tourist hotspots for their sheer remoteness, only ... well, they are now packed with tourists. Remoteness is now something you'll only find – as we found – if you come here at the crack of dawn. Strange.

Just next to the Silfra Ridge is the site of the Althing – the meeting place of Iceland's parliament (the oldest in the world). Chosen, I guess, because it's central, so easy for all the far-flung regions of the Vikingdom (you can have that) to reach. Here they would camp and spend two weeks each summer debating laws, adjudicating cases, swapping stories, trading animals and other commodities, swimming in the glacial waters of the lakes and rivers, performing religious rites, eating food from stalls, drinking, dancing, shagging and carrying out strange mystical acts (or any combination of the above).

Essentially it was a fortnight of Glastonbury, with a pinch of the *Moral Maze*, *Call You And Yours* and a whack of Crufts thrown in for good measure. It all took place at the ridge, at the very point where the two land masses meet, one – as we've already discovered – a convenient 10 metres higher than the other, thus creating the perfect wall for the lawmaker to stand in front of so that his words might resonate and reach the ears of all the people. This is the point from which the whole of Iceland seems to have grown – the crack from which the magma has spilt out and spread. Those old Icelanders certainly had a hell of a sense of place. I am tempted to hang around and soak it all up – not least so I can try out the acoustics with a blast of song, if only there were a gap in the endless procession of tourists – but the cold has now started to get into my marrow, and my extremities are in danger of becoming Mattin-worthy photograph subjects. We scurry back to the car and wallow hungrily in the warmth.

8

Orri Vigfússon: Salmon Stock Saviour

Shortly before leaving home for the frozen North, I caught up with my good friend Chris Watson – a lovely former neighbour from the not-so-frozen expanse of north London tundra that the Viking invaders called 'Islington'. So many Sunday afternoons over the years have been rescued from freewheeling into school-night torpor by Chris's kind invitation to hop over the wall and drink his wine – and it always was Chris's wine, not just because he is extremely generous and had an enviable cellar but also because it literally was his wine. He actually made the stuff – he has a vineyard in Burgundy from which an exceptionally good white comes year after year, always labelled with the same print of a tower from which two children (Chris's eldest two, Emma and Alex) peer out of the windows. I remember very clearly the night Chris came round to tell me that David Heyman, the producer of the *Harry Potter* films, had called to say that Chris's daughter had just been given the part of Hermione. Wonder what happened to her . . .

Anyway, Chris emailed me an introduction to a friend of his called Orri Vigfússon and insisted that I get in touch with him when in Iceland. We've settled into rather a lovely institutionalized rhythm, tending to rise very early to get off to our filming, work an intensive day and return to our hotel rooms to unwind, catch up with emails, read a little, ring home and in my case write up this journal. Then we meet up for dinner, usually in our hotel or somewhere nearby, before an early night so we can get up in time to repeat the whole shebang in the morning. It's rather a hermetic existence – especially for a team making an exploratory documentary – but the routine becomes rather comforting. Having made contact with Orri, he has kindly said I must give him an evening when I'm in Reykjavik so he can show me around. I'm appalled to admit that I have strange misgivings about stepping outside our safe little production bubble. But then again Chris, from whom nothing but good flows, has said I have to meet him, so I can't really opt out.

I momentarily grow up enough to send Orri an email, and a plan is duly made to meet in the hotel's reception that night and go out for dinner. I head down to meet him, suddenly remembering that our hotel's lobby is the size of a small village and generally has a commensurate population. Orri doesn't know me and I don't know him, but, curiously, I pad about the various corners of the reception quite certain that I'll know him from the sixty-odd other potential Orris on offer. And then, just when I'm thinking what a stupid basis this is for finding anyone, there in front of me is the man who is incontrovertibly Orri. He's on the telephone at reception – clearly ringing my room – and when I step up and say 'Orri?', he puts down the telephone and smiles. Turns out I was right: of course I'd know Orri when I saw him. Apart from anything else he's the only person in reception in a smart tweed jacket. And to think he blinked first, having to telephone my room . . .

Literally the first thing you notice on meeting Orri is that you like him: he's a man in his sixties, short, quite stocky, but glowing with health, with thick silver hair and the kind of avuncular, twinkly face that lets you know you are in extremely good company. Over the course of the next three hours I rather come to revere Orri – he's not just good company, he's also something of a hero. He tells me about how he and Chris know each other. Orri, it turns out, is a salmon conservationist who has made it his life's goal to halt the years of depressing decline in North Atlantic salmon stocks. He goes about this by buying out, one by one, all the netters on as many North Sea/North Atlantic rivers as possible. This, I quickly discover, is typical of the man; he doesn't seek to ban netting – that's not his style and, besides, he appreciates that the netters need to make a living – instead, he buys them off. Netting is the practice of spreading huge nets across salmon rivers during the salmon season and hauling out humungous volumes of them as they journey upwater to spawn. Orri negotiates personally with every single one he comes across, agrees a price at which they're happy to stop all netting activity (in some cases he even brings the netsmen round to the side of the angels to work in the cause of salmon conservation), and the results, fishery by fishery, are beginning to show.

He's been at it for twenty-five years and bit by bit, year by year, the decline has been slowed to the point where there are now grounds for optimism that it may even be reversed. One day, in our lifetimes perhaps, there might once again be plentiful wild salmon running up the rivers of the North Atlantic. Why do we still have to be taught about conservation, though? Why, after hundreds and hundreds of years of careful management, have we lost sight of the basic contract between us and our habitat? It's kind of embarrassing when you see the gentle expertise of Orri with his salmon mission, or Børge (*Ja! Ja!*) with his skrei and his coffee mug, to think how far astray we've allowed ourselves to be led by noisier commercial interests. If you hoik out stupidly massive quantities of the things, they will eventually run out: it's perfectly simple. The deal is you protect the shoal and the habitat, and you can take what you need from the stock – all you have to do is keep the merest thought for the future at the back of your mind. I do sometimes wonder if our occasional obsession with doomsday scenarios, those stories that Sunday papers love to run that can be anything from imminent global pandemic to meteor collision to soaring climate change to a fatal rash of house price rises (*Mail on Sunday*), mightn't be one of the reasons we make such meagre provision for future generations. Has our sense of where we are on the trajectory of human existence started to erode what should be an innate need to preserve and build for the future? Or have I been drinking too much coffee?

The west coast of Scotland is speckled with huge salmon farms from which come poor, insipid specimens of the fish, grown to maturity in cages, often fed horrific pap that doses them with additives to colour their flesh a deeper, more enticing pink, or laces them with prophylactic doses of antibiotics. There are of course farmed salmon that are organic, which means they're fed organic pap (the best kind!), but they still spend their lives in cages. Tragically, this is pretty much the only salmon available to us because it is very simply and cheaply sourced. And this terrible glut of cheap factory-salmon – only a couple of steps away from food grown on a petri dish, when all's said and done – has distracted us from the wild salmon's dwindling numbers. The wild salmon's life is so exotically migratory (each fish swims thousands of miles every year up to the coast of Greenland to feed then comes back to the river of its birth all silvered from its time at sea) that it's hard to think of a greater cruelty than to keep this creature caged. It is truly heartening to hear about Orri's campaign.

Orri knows EVERY river – not just the A-list rivers like the Tweed or the Findhorn or the Tamar or the Towy but the tiny ones like our lovely Coquet in Northumberland, even the little stretch below our farm from Pauperhaugh down to Brinkburn Priory, where we spent every summer of our childhood fishing for little brown trout and hurling ourselves in on hot days. Orri knows every inch and every landowner and every water authority on this and every river of corresponding size not just in England, not just in the UK, nor just in Northern Europe but right across that whole portion of the globe that feeds into the North Atlantic. And in each place I would bet my life there are hundreds of people whose faces brighten at the name of Orri Vigfússon.

Orri shows me a bit more of Reykjavik, including the opera house of which he is the proud chairman. I have been rather harsh on Reykjavik it seems. There's a small enclave of the old town which has immense character and charm, full of what I assume is the local architectural vernacular: houses, not so much timbered as covered in painted corrugated iron, but in a rather fetching pale cream colour. It's extremely attractive, just a shame they didn't continue a bit more in that vein rather than swiftly moving on to the Shankill Road look.

So thank you, Chris. If I ever get to do more expeditions, I promise not to sit in my room every night. I will make it my business to spend every other night (let's not go nuts) going out and meeting friends of friends.

For our next trip, we're off up to the second-largest glacier in Iceland (in fact the second largest in Europe, that's how blingingly glacier-rich this place is. Any way you care to look at it, Iceland was the perfect name for it) to visit an ice cave being dug out there. It's really just a tourist attraction. They have so many tourists in Iceland they are actually falling over themselves to find new things to show them. Reykjavik is putting up new hotels faster than they can think of places for the coachfuls to visit, but the idea of an ice cave does seem particularly bonkers. We drive for about two hours from the capital then jump into two specially converted eight-wheelers ('Converted from what?' I ask. 'Oh, they were NATO missile launchers before; they came here from Poland') that drive us up the glacier to a height of 1,200 metres.

These are impressive conveyances, though. Each of the eight shoulder-height wheels has a complicated hose system coming out of it, like the greenhouse at someone's second home, linking it to a computer that monitors and changes the tyre pressures to suit the terrain. Every so often there's a hiss as the onboard computer lets air out of the tyres so they can 'float over the snow'. Trouble is, the higher you get the lower the atmospheric pressure, so we end up constantly leaking air behind us (much as I sometimes do when skiing). For all the tech, though, we move across and up the glacier at the pace of a stately slug. The ice cave, which we eventually reach after about three hours of uphill big-wheeling, is utterly surrounded by a flat landscape of snow and ice as far as the eye can see. Finally we've come to the very landscape my children think I'm living in the whole time I'm away. The site is surrounded by yellow diggers and swarms of builders in the time-honoured 'deadline-approaching' phase of construction. I am very much hoping that after three hours on the launcher there is something here for us to see.

There is, but my hunch was dead right: the ice cave is nuts. They've dug 600 metres into the glacier to make a looping tunnel that brings you around in a perfect underground horseshoe 500 metres long from end to end. We walk in at the cave mouth and burrow down under the glacier until we're about 40 metres below the surface. The tunnels are beautiful, striated with layers of compressed snow. Already, the ice cave has done one valuable thing (apart from providing an excuse for us to ride a couple of missile launchers up a mountain); it has finally managed to do what years of geography lessons never did: it has taught me what a glacier is. Allow me to explain. Glaciers are made up of the snow that doesn't melt each year (in the Arctic you've got to guess that to be about 99 per cent of the snow that falls), which builds year on year, gets compressed by subsequent years' snow, and creates something like the rings on trees. Down beneath the ice, the tunnels feel like they're carved out of the purest stripy humbug, each stripe around me representing another year of snowfall. As the stripes are forced further and further down the pile by the next year's snowfall, they get more and more compressed. Siggi the guide points out the layer from 2010, the year of the famous eruption of the catchily named volcano Eyjafjallajökull (which rhymes quite niftily with 'Angela Merkel', if anyone's desperately keen to put it in a limerick). This is an unusually thick grey-black layer, which suggests how hellish it must have been in Iceland at the time. Forget all our cancelled flights from Benidorm; they were suffocating beneath a thick blanket of doom.

Guess what? Down at the bottom of the strange circle of the cave's humbug passage there's a chapel. I'm guessing it's for weddings – pretty sure they don't have choral evensong at this one either. But I'm beginning to enjoy this neo-Renaissance idea of having a chapel in these new tourist attractions; all they need now is some court composers and they're away . . . The ice cave is certainly a strange place. I would find the total madness of it as an idea quite appealing if only its *raison d'être* weren't so transparently (translucently) mercantile. It's a bit like digging an enormous hole in the ground on Exmoor so you can open Hole World and charge families £100 a visit. Actually that's not a bad idea . . .

Spirits rise on the journey home, partly because progress back to the cars is about twenty times faster coming downhill and partly because on the way we finally discover how to listen to MP3s in our car instead of Radio Iceland. It's not that I don't enjoy the local sounds, it's just that they're not actually all that local and, besides, we've been away for a bit now and are starting to feel the need for some home tunes. I set myself up as DJ and play tracks from everyone's various music libraries all the way back to Reykjavik. Dominic the director's library is full of Music I Once Owned On Tape But Haven't Bothered Buying Again For My iPod, so we sing along to Ry Cooder and then throw ourselves on David Gray's *White Ladder*, before remembering that 'Please Forgive Me' and 'Babylon' are probably the only songs we need concern ourselves with. Adrienne, our charming French assistant producer for the Iceland/Greenland leg of the journey, has an obligingly 'Fransh' playlist of Jacques Brel and Charles Aznavour, so we pep up the set list with a little '*Valse à Mille Temps*'. For some reason all my music is on the iCloud (I bet Ranulph Fiennes doesn't make such schoolboy errors), so I can only play the tiny handful of tracks that my phone has randomly bothered to download.

Radio Iceland would be a lot more listenable to if it played less generic global pop and more local product. They're a musical lot in these parts – in Iceland every child has to learn an instrument all the way through school (in the same way that the rest of us learn maths). The result seems to be massively talented musicians at every level – I'm not sure what the impact is on their general numeracy, but I doubt that the economic crash of 2011 can be attributed to an excess of trombone lessons. Either way, singers and producers from Iceland are now renowned the world over. I suppose Björk is their Bob Marley in that regard (and there are two names you don't often see in the same sentence). As a further index of its cultural vitality, Iceland is also the world's most literate nation in per capita terms. They're avid readers and writers (hence the bookshops and libraries being packed until late each night).

As is becoming the norm, our flight out of Iceland is delayed by twenty-four hours due to the storm that blows up on our third day here (they call it a tornado, but there seems to be little evidence of that kind of caper), so we have to move out to a new hotel next to the airport, as there are ten thousand more tourists scheduled to arrive at our old one. One of the problems with so much of Reyjkavik looking like the kind of buildings that spring up around airports is that it is therefore really bloody hard to find the actual airport. The 'Reykjavik' airport we flew into when we arrived was miles and miles away from Reykjavik. This one, which is commendably close to Reykjavik (as far as we can tell), must be the domestic airport, but I'm beginning to suspect our satnav lady is a little tipsy as she leads us a merry dance around a great many places that would be ideal siting for an airport but are just missing the all important 'terminal' element these places seem to require. Strangely, the authorities have gone to almost wartime lengths to keep the airport's precise whereabouts a secret – there are no signs of any kind. Eventually – and I mean after driving down likely but wrong turnings for over an hour and trying every conceivable turn-off, how-ever preposterous – we stumble on it and there, sure enough, is the hotel, where a man with plucked eyebrows and a downturned mouth grudgingly checks us in. I have rather liked all the Icelanders I've met so far but suddenly come to realize how much I miss the reliably upbeat out-look of the Norwegians.

Our journey the following morning will eventually take four of us (Adrienne is travelling on to the following location to do some recceing) to Constable Point on the east coast of Greenland, such a barren and isolated outpost that our only hope of getting there is by chartering our own flight. Charter flights only leave from Akureyri on the north coast of Iceland. So we hop on the early-morning scheduled flight up to Akureyri on what is essentially a flying bus. Our boarding cards are just small betting slips, each with slightly differing odds, so we stand at the departure gate (Gate 1 of 1) holding our slips and gazing up at the screen like we're in a pub on Grand National day.

At Akureyri, where we are laid up for a further four hours, I spot my new friend Orri from a couple of nights before making his way into the terminal having just landed from Reykjavik on a later flying bus. Just like in Svalbard I am getting the sense that if you wait in an airport terminal for a couple of hours you'll probably bump into most of the people you've met. Delighted to see Orri again, I stand to catch his attention, but as soon as he sets foot in the terminal about twenty others have also risen to their feet, and delighted shouts of 'Orri!' go up from every corner. It's a bit like being at some eighteenth-century court – especially for Orri himself, as he isn't allowed out of the place until he's spoken to and shaken hands with nearly everyone in the terminal. I quickly recalibrate my estimation of Orri. The man's clearly some kind of national hero – and so he should be: every country needs its Orris.

A little twin otter plane eventually lands on the strip outside, and its two pilots make their way over to talk us through the flight plan to Greenland. This is clearly the next level of care that comes with a private charter. We sagely approve the pilots' flight plan as if it makes the first modicum of sense to us, and we are ready to go. The last formality before leaving Icelandic sovereign territory is to visit the Akureyri Duty Free, which is being specially opened in our honour (this being a rare non-domestic flight). We get a bottle of whisky and some beers. The pilots buy as much as they can carry and can be feasibly contained within the limits of a twin otter's cockpit space without pressing against too many buttons on the dash.

We bid a fond farewell to Akureyri, particularly to the man behind the counter at the airport cafe who has become a close friend during our lay-up. I don't know if they have darts in Iceland, but I have never met a person who looks more suited to the sport. His face, his clothes, his build, his walk, his moustache, all speak of the arrers. When this man and darts finally meet, the heat and light given off will be awesome – perhaps on a level with that original eruption which first created this remarkable island. He also has a way with smoked-salmon sandwiches that brings a tear to the eye . . .

9

You Can Be Sirius: On Patrol With Danish Special Forces

The twin otter flies bravely north for three hours to the cold unknown of Constable Point. After only half an hour of flying, the sea below us begins to appear ice-strewn, as if an aeroplane carrying the world's largest cargo of Kendal Mint Cake has forgotten to close its aft doors. The morsels of ice grow more and more numerous until they first gather together like huge islands of rubbish are wont to do at sea, then bind together into a harlequin patchwork of sea ice. As we approach the east coast of Greenland, mountains rise up out of the shelf of ice and we see actual evidence of land beneath. The earth seems to perform a terrestrial burlesque as you go north – by the time you get to Greenland, she's flung all but the sparsest greenery away and is quite naked but modestly

Aerial view of Norway's lovely Lofoten Islands.

Step aside, Royal Marines, this 'making fire for the camera' is a job for a real man.

Be kind to your twin prop and (hopefully) your twin prop will be kind to you.

Bedding down at the Ice Hotel is a pretty seductive business, as I'm sure all you ladies will agree.

In the eye of the Kiruna ice storm.

With Børge and his catch – you should've seen the one that got away.

Ice Swimming – the clue is in the name.

Top-flight skidoo action –
technically this could be a
still from the next Bond film.

Living out all my 'man at the wheel of
an improbably large vehicle' fantasies
via a Tromsø snow clearer.

Sharing yet another moment of
unrestrained levity with Alexander
Pilditch.

Snorkelling between tectonic plates.

I hate to think what Len Goodman would've made of my polka.

Descending to the ice cave with Siggi.

Fur-hatted man notices looming iceberg.

A man alone, striding bravely into the unknown, with only a five-man crew and a series of luxury hotel reservations to sustain him in his heroic fight against the elements.

The Sirius guys generously waive headband and facial hair entry requirements to welcome their newest recruit.

hung about with snow and ice in all the right places.

The pilots, who keep up a genial banter during the whole three hours we're in the air (clearly excited about their booze bonanza at Akureyri and itching to pull a stopper or two out with their teeth and sing air shanties all the way back to Iceland – that's what pilots do when we're not there, isn't it?), turn back to announce excitedly that we are approaching Constable Point: 'There's your destination!' We crane our necks around the little porthole windows to see where we're heading. Ah, and there it is: Constable Point, a woebegone collection of red-painted corrugated-iron Nissen huts and a windsock.

We land on something remarkably like a runway (a piece of flat ice that has been cleared for the purpose and marked out with a couple of lights here and there) and taxi up to the largest of the corrugated-iron barns. We climb down from the plane and load our luggage and thousand cases on to a big orange trolley, and a jovial, fleshy fellow marches over.

'Hi! I'm Robert.' Handshakes all round. 'I've just replaced Heinrich as airport manager. He left this morning, so I'll be looking after you. I'm in charge for the next five weeks. You wanna go drop off your luggage, you can take it now.' He points a generous finger towards a low-lying bit of barn about 200 yards away on the edge of the – I want to call it airport complex, but it's not really either an airport or especially complex, more a cluster of single-storey buildings made, as I say, out of corrugated iron . . . nothing complex about that. Imagine a farm with a landing strip and a little bit of prefab classroom block tacked on and you've got it. 'You're over there,' he concludes.

We trundle the big orange trolley over the shiniest, slipperiest compacted snow we've yet come across in these northern parts (hilariously, all of us fall over; some, even more hilariously, several times) and come to the 'hotel' end of the set-up. The sign next to the door has the famous Hilton logo on it, but where the stars usually line up, here they are blank, hollow stars, and to the left of the five hollow stars is one painted yellow with a −1 next to it. The door next to the sign is so completely frozen and drifted with snow there is no way anyone can get through it, so we edge round the building until we find a side door − also drifted up with snow, but it's at least possible to climb up the drift and over the icy banister to open the door.

Inside, it smells like school. There's a short poky corridor off which are small cells, each with a bunk bed built into its corner and a scrap of material hanging down to cover the window pane in perfect imitation of a curtain. At the end of the corridor is a common room with a sink and some old (again think school) sofas and a coffee table (only without 'Church is a berk' carved into it as it would have − indeed did have − at my school), some bookcases on which are lined up bumper novels by people called things like Scrān Djhæmmerskjøld and, curiously, a tray of cooked penne pasta and a casserole dish full of stew, both of which must have been there for days if not weeks but thanks to the fridge-like cold of the place seem almost edible (which is oddly more revolting than if they were growing feathers – as if perhaps you might almost eat them by mistake). They remain untouched either by us or the cleaning staff for the duration of our stay.

Beyond is a large washroom with a separate loo at the back. Of course (of course) there's no sewage at Constable Point (where would it go?), so all (both) the loos are just seats with large heavy-duty (at least you've got to hope) black plastic bags beneath to gather everything that falls into them, but there's no polite flushing or covering or indeed anything between you and what nappy recyclers like to call 'the insult' of previous users. You'd imagine we might be wrinkling our noses up and longing to be else-where, but strangely – possibly because there's no alternative, or maybe because the –1 star outside had pre-pared us – there's no murmur of complaint from any quarter. In fact in a funny way it's kind of cosy.

We are here at Constable Point to join Danish special forces out on the Sirius Patrol. Greenland has been inhabited for somewhere between four and five thousand years – originally by Arctic peoples of what would now be called Canadian origin, then by Norse colonists between the tenth and fifteenth centuries, with the Inuits arriving somewhere near the middle of that period. Needless to say, it was Europeans who finally decided they owned the place, and competing territorial claims between Denmark and Norway persisted long after Greenland officially became a Danish colony in 1814 (and even once it had been enshrined – or ensnared, depending on your point of view – as part of the Danish realm in the constitution of 1953).

Even though it was officially Denmark's territory, Norwegian whalers and trappers never stopped coming to the east coast of this huge island – proportionately the world's least populous country. And while in recent years a succession of referendums (or referenda, if you'd prefer, although that sounds a bit like someone's exotic au pair) have taken the Greenlanders ever closer to full independence, they're still technically a protectorate of the Danish Crown. So Denmark maintains its sovereignty by literally walking Greenland's perimeters to keep an eye out for pesky Norwegian interlopers.

The Sirius Patrol is made up of six two-man units, each with a sled and thirteen dogs, a tent, a stack of ration packs, and, um, that's it. These guys are Sirius (shoot me). They come to Greenland for twenty-six months, severing all but the most rudimentary contact with home, family, friends and girlfriends. They build their two-man sled as part of their training and then are sent out into the desolate wilds of Greenland's eastern region, where they drive it for six hours a day, covering 30–40 km, then they pitch camp at 4 p.m., tend to the dogs, radio in to base to say that they haven't seen any Norwegians so far, cook and eat some supper and generally subsist in temperatures that range from –60° on a bad day to –15° on a good.

We are joining the patrol for twenty-four hours – finally spending our time in a way that ex-Major in the Marines Paul Mattin would consider a plausible Arctic activity.

Back at the base, having decided who gets which bunk (we toss a coin, Coat of Arms or Fish; I go Arms because it's most of my surname, and lose) and we halve the size of our rooms simply by bringing our bags into them. Then we go over to the canteen 500 yards away on the other side of the airport/rink. Constable Point is a base of the kind that will be familiar to any ex-forces personnel. Subsistence and luxury aren't that far away from each other really; as long as there's hot food and enough of it, warmth, a bed, a basin, somewhere to plug your various electrical things in and a sturdy black bag behind a lockable door, you've got everything covered. What more could you possibly want?

It takes us no time at all to become utterly institutionalized; after seventy-two hours on base we will be completely up to speed with the canteen's opening hours and how it is organized, where we find the school knives and forks sticking up from their big pots, how the washing-up system works. We will even become friendly with the chef (a sinister blend of Boris Yeltsin and a furious Benny Hill) and exchange chatty pleasantries with the various other inhabitants of the base – truly a trifle of many ingredients, including airport staff (the sponge), maintenance people (custard), cleaners (jelly) and meteorologists (the overwhelming sherry) – but for now it all feels a bit like we've arrived in a disaster movie set on an international space station.

It's here at Constable Point that we get our first clear sight of the striking ethnic leap between Northern European and Inuit. Our journey north has taken us to the roots of Norse culture. Up here at the very wellspring of Celtic DNA, we've seen all the archetypes of historic Northern European appearance – Fat Nick Clegg and Fatt Damon and Chubby Jamie Oliver. In Iceland, throw in Boris Becker and any other person you can think of with blue eyes and pale eyelashes and you get an idea of how little this gene pool has been stirred over the years. But those Celts are the indigenous people in those parts – they're aboriginals. For once they're not there as colonists or imperious over-lords; this is where this appearance originates from.

It's unsurprising but still worth noting that there is none of the ethnic diversity of the UK up at this latitude – in the days we were there I didn't see a single black person in Iceland, where the only ethnic variation was provided by the coaches of Chinese tourists. In Norway there are Muslim communities – many Balkan refugees went there in the nineties – but it's striking how white the general population is. Then in Greenland, just as you've got used to the increasing Aryan-ness of everyone as you travel further and further north, Bang! You're into a whole new and exciting ethnicity: the Inuit!

With no warning at all, the indigenous population has switched from being big-boned, blond, pudgy-faced chef lookalikes to having a Nepali/Mongolian appearance. It is suddenly thrillingly international. And you begin to understand that all these northern countries that used to seem worlds away from each other on the old Mercator projection of the world actually huddle together like a scrummage at the top of the round Earth.

* * *

We meet the Sirius boys in the canteen. Let's just try to imagine, shall we, what these Danish special forces dudes might be like: guys who sign up to live almost alone on the ice for twenty-six months of their lives. In my mind's eye they are bull-necked Ross Kemp types or lantern-jawed army sorts who take things desperately seriously and who like as not will have no truck whatsoever with noncey media people like us. What we discover is quite surprising: it turns out the two utterly charming, affable and easy-going people we fall into conversation with while waiting for the Sirius meatheads to rock up are actually . . . well, yes, you'll have guessed it by now.

Both in their twenties, Caspar and Tobias are normal build, although doing the patrol has made them whip sharp: there isn't a spare ounce of meat on either of them. But in lieu of that spare meat there is an awful of lot of hair. Tobias wears his shoulder length and has a cracking beard that must be a good three or four inches long. He completes the look with a bandana tied around his head. Caspar has more of a goatee beard, but both of them give off a kind of 'Nam vet/surfer vibe and are instantly friendly. This twenty-four hours out with them is suddenly looking a good deal more fun.

The Constable Point canteen, which is the beating heart of the base, runs along strict military lines. Supper, for example, is at 1800 hrs, after which Erasmus (a Danish officer from the Arctic Joint Command who has come along to help with the filming) says there will be a briefing (at 'about' 1900 hrs). We all gather in the common room in the hotel and Raz (as I suspect he's not called) comes in carrying a large sheaf of papers. He starts his briefing with a bit about the history of the patrol, of Greenland, then of Greenland during the war, of Norway and Greenland, then Denmark and Greenland, the dates of various agreements and much, much more.

After he has been speaking for nearly twenty-five minutes, I spot Raz take the top sheet off his sheaf and lay it on the table. My eyes flick down and casually notice that this sheet carries all the bullet points he's just been talking about. Oh hell. The second sheet, sure enough, has as its title the very thing he's literally just said. This is no briefing: it's a longing. He must have at least twenty bits of paper in his stack. At this rate we're going to be here for heaven knows how many hundred hours. Anyway, I learn a lot during the talk, useful things like the fact that Danes spell out the years in English as much as they can, so 1947 becomes 'nineteen hundred and forty-seven', like it's the grand total raised by a jumble sale. Also – although this could just be Erasmus's thing – if something lasted several years they'll refer to the dates backwards, so the First World War was from nineteen hundred and eighteen to nineteen hundred and fourteen. It all adds to the fun, of course, but does leave me wondering if it really will all be over by Christmas. The other fascinating discovery I make is that Danish has a subliminal Liverpudlian inflection. In the same way I had a eureka moment listening to Norwegians and hearing Geordie, Erasmus's speech is pure Scouse.

Eventually we turn in for our first night in the −1 star Hilton. I sleep surprisingly well and really don't mind the musty-smelling sheets and pillows, nor even the lumpy top bunk of the bed. It's just like every holiday of my childhood – all that's missing is the smell of mothballs. It's like the cosiest night imaginable, with an Arctic wind howling outside. I daresay we should make the most of it, as this time tomorrow it'll be us out there in the freezing wilds.

The patrol leaves bright and early, and up here early is – like 'all things' in the hymn – bright and beautiful. We have a rather more leisurely morning before following their tracks and joining them by skidoo at around lunchtime along with three men (who turned up from nowhere) from a 'local' tour equipment company who are providing our skidoos and the tents and sleeping bags we'll be using later. On arrival at their sled I am kitted out with ski boots, but special ones for Nordic skiing, so the heel isn't fixed. It's surprising how very different this feels to the sensation of a regular ski boot that sits rigidly in its ski (and, moreover, snaps out of it with ease). I stand up like a drunk and gingerly take a few steps. The idea is you hold on to a rope at the back of the sled and either slide or slide-walk in a Nordic way as the mood takes you. Most dog sledding involves standing or sitting on the sled as it goes along, but this method was devised specially for the Sirius so that the patrollers don't get cold. It was well devised: after doing it for five minutes my core temperature is way up in the paint cards. If this keeps up, I'm going to have to take off one of my nine layers. I vaguely remember ex-Major in the

Marines Paul Mattin saying that the one thing you must avoid is sweating, as sweat then freezes and that – in the way of so many Mattin tales – 'can get a bit gnarly'.

The dogs are strung out in front in a line, chained in pairs. They are very sweet and extremely affectionate (which is all the more surprising given that they sleep out in all temperatures and have the strength of ten men). The boys shout commands at them, and the dogs respond straight away. Ish. '*Hunde clar!*' seems to be the cry to get things underway, and the dogs leap into a pulling frenzy. '*Hulle hulle*' means 'Whoaaaa there, boy', and 'Howser Bowser' evidently means cool your jets.

We speed off (at about 30 kmh), with the newest recruit making what seems initially to be good progress. Then we come to a bit where rocks start poking out of the snow. Of course the skis don't really slide over rock that well and so as soon as I hit one, over I tumble, skis and all (the boys seem to have a technique for dealing with rock underfoot whereby they kind of run on their skis from foot to foot, so if one sticks the other can quickly take up the strain), and then I desperately scrabble about trying to get back on to my feet. This is one of the things the patrol boys can't afford to do, at the risk of losing the sled, the dogs, their shelter and warmth, and all their provisions. If the dogs are inclined to, they might just rush off on a whim without the patrol attached. There's a thick coil of knotted rope that can occasionally be slung around the runners to slow down the sled, but it's by no means failsafe, as the dogs can still pull an unmanned sled with a knotted rope on its runners for up to 15 km before they'll get tired and give up.

There's also a longer rope that runs from behind the sled so that should either of the boys fall off they can grab hold of that and pull themselves back on. While we're watching, I see a couple of moments when even these seasoned and conditioned pros have to hurl themselves at the sled so it doesn't run away without them. Part of their training is to get to a base – never more than 100 km away (which doesn't sound like much until you think about how far it actually is) – on skis alone, so if they ever do lose their sled that is where they head.

We slide on with me holding on to the back for about three hours. The sun occasionally glimmers through the clouds but mostly it's a flat light that doesn't really show up the contours of the snow we're gliding over. This is phenomenal exercise. I can feel all sorts of muscles I haven't used for years getting a decent workover. Satisfyingly I even seem to be getting the hang of the half skiing/half walking. This is great – I reckon I can't have fallen arse over tit more than about twenty times before we reach the place where we are to set up camp for the night.

The boys take it in turn to be Outside Man or Inside Man. Both of them get the tent up (this takes them about twenty seconds – very impressive) then Outside Man collects snow for Inside Man so he can start melting it for drinking and cooking, then tends to the dogs and sets up anchors with the skis to keep both the dogs and the sled in place overnight. Meanwhile, Inside Man gets the stove lit and the snow melting going and starts making supper. The stove is an incredibly efficient and vital piece of their kit. It acts as heater and clothes dryer as well as cooker. By the time we come into the tent (ten minutes after it went up), it is so wonderfully hot that everyone can sit comfortably in T-shirts despite the –30 howling-gale scenario outside.

This is how the boys manage to keep body and soul together. The tent each evening is a home and a very cosy (even luxurious) one at that. It's funny how you start to feel an almost childlike attachment to warmth in these punishing temperatures; you attach yourself to it and suck every last bit of nourishment from it. I remember when I came back to the car from the snorkelling with winky Kevin he passed me his mittens to put on my blue fingers, and there was something so indescribably wonderful about the thick downy pom-pommy warmth of those gloves. The sheer comfort of them in the howling gale and driving snow made me think primal thoughts of being held in my mother's arms as a mewling and puking infant. Quite bizarre, but when I mentioned it later to the crew there were several nods of recognition. One or two of them even smiled kindly before grimacing at each other when they thought I couldn't see: a sure sign they completely agreed.

Supper is rather extraordinary – surprisingly delicious – and ready in no time at all. Caspar just adds boiling water to a bag and suddenly magics up chilli con carne, which just as promptly magics away again down my fat throat. Once the food is devoured, we chat about the boys' time with the patrol and how they manage to get on so well for long, long months at a time. 'Well, they choose us to be people who can get on and who are also happy in our own company.' These were two well-chosen candidates on that score. How often do they see other people? 'Every six weeks or so we might stay at a base and there's usually someone else there. We can email home, Skype or whatever, get some new books . . .' Ah yes, the Scrān Djhæmmerskjøld library. The Sirius Patrol have books in every little hut along the way so that the patrollers can replenish their reading stocks as they go.

'You must become incredibly close friends,' I say, 'or not.'

'Of course, you become very close. You have to have a very honest relationship and make sure you share everything; anything that you want to say is best said out loud and not stored up.' The boys both agree. 'But,' adds Caspar, 'the thing you notice about Sirius people is that they are reflective, contemplative. They don't talk all the time.'

Do you ration out your conversation? 'Well, you've got a lot of time, so you're gonna get to hear all the other guy's jokes, all his conversation topics, you're gonna get to know all his friends and family by name. For one year you're gonna be closer to that guy than anyone else has ever been.'

So what happens when you both go back to Copenhagen – is it heartbreaking to say goodbye to someone who's shared so much with you?

'Yeah, it's pretty sad, but you make sure you see each other from time to time.'

If little strains of the *Brokeback Mountain* music are itching to make themselves heard in my head, they aren't quite finding resonance. There is something so guileless and honest about two men in their twenties being able to discuss a bond of friendship as strong as this without making light of it, or feeling they even have to acknowledge the nudge-nudge naughty-postcard interpretation that has become the first instinct of the British. We love innuendo so much we'll even truffle it out of perfectly innocent circumstances (Oi oi? A vicar? He MUST be banging some choirboy behind the altar. Two men out on patrol sharing a tent? They MUST be hanging out the back of each other). But that is why these people were chosen – not because they were army meatheads but because they knew their minds, were good at ordering their thoughts and thus were judged to be the kind of people who could survive in the wild for long stretches of time. I would imagine the greatest danger to life on the Sirius Patrol would otherwise be one of the patrollers garrotting the other with a guy rope.

I do begin to see what the allure of Sirius is: the combination of discipline and complete freedom and the unexpected sense of ownership you are given of the wildest and most beautiful landscape on the planet. It's pitted against you, and your survival depends on your mastery of it, but if you can do it – and you only get the gig if you can – then the thrill of all that icy self-reliance must be overwhelming. Throw in the moon and stars above and the Northern Lights (which they must see so much it probably gets boring), along with thirteen utterly devoted dogs (all of which have names and personalities – Amundsen often kept himself going on his three-year trip to find the Northwest Passage by tuning in to the constant soap opera of the dogs' lives. It was, he said, utterly compelling, and I should think a very good way of distracting yourself when everything else got a bit much), and the whole experience must be mind-blowing . . . and (Oi oi?) you get to cosy up for a bit of man love every night, eh? Eh? Ha ha! Man love! Oi oi!

Supper is soon over and it's still only 5.30. My tent has been provided by our new tour-company friends and so isn't (strangely) anything like as clever as the one Caspar and Tobias have – it's essentially the sort of tent you camp at the bottom of the garden in till about 10.30 then go inside because you're scared. The tour company haven't thought to provide any stove for my tent, which is odd (given that temperatures will be in the −30s overnight). You never sleep with the stove/heater burning, for fire- and carbon-monoxide-related reasons, but it's very useful for making the interior of the tent into somewhere you might want to sit for those hours between putting the tent up and turning out the light.

'Oh no!' the guide insists. 'You don't need a stove. No one has stoves!' Well, I notice he'd certainly put one in for himself . . . In the event, the Sirius boys have a spare Primus, which is truly hopeless – I'd have got more heat from a burning match – but still a great deal better than nothing and takes the edge off the searing cold of my tent's interior (I reckon I get it down to a balmy −5 in there – mmmmmm). I turn in at about 6.30, hoping to kill a bit of time reading my Kindle, only to discover that a) of course you can't read a Kindle in gloves and b) somewhat irritatingly, my tent is made out of the crinkliest, thinnest polyurethane (you know those really crackly old Argos carrier bags? It is that kind of crinkly), and the storm that is blowing up outside is making a truly alarming noise with it. There are a couple of moments in that very long night when I actually don't think I am going to blow away.

At about half past eight, just when I'm thinking of attempting sleep and just after the Sirius boys have radioed in to base ('No Norwegians so far, but the chilli con carne went down quite well'), Tobias calls out, 'Northern Lights!' So I worm my way out of my sleeping bag, pull on as many layers as I can and unzip the tent – it's worth pointing out that all this takes about fifteen minutes; it just does. There's no doing anything without going through the ceremony of keeping out the cold and, in a tent, that takes three times longer than otherwise. Fleeces, coats, inner gloves, outer gloves, inner boots, outer boots, try to open the tent, take off outer gloves, try again, take off inner gloves, open tent, put on all gloves . . . watch Northern Lights.

Bloody hell! This is exciting. We've searched for the Northern Lights ever since we've come to the Arctic in all the places the local guides say are the best for seeing them – Kiruna, Tromsø, Kirkenes, Svalbard . . . and here they are out in the middle of nowhere in Greenland with just us and two tents and thirteen dogs. Not a Northern Lights expert in sight. Ha! Where are you now, Astrid?

They are subtle, on account of the moon, which isn't quite full but full enough – and bright enough – to dim the lights a bit, but they are still extraordinarily beautiful. I obviously know – God knows it's been hammered into me often enough – that they're not caused by spirits of the dead dancing or by the gods' displeasure and it's just the solar winds coming into the atmosphere. But it is SOOO utterly mesmerizing: the channels the light particles choose to follow, the swirl, the way swells of colour gradually and then unmistakably appear in other zones of the sky with no warning. It's such a wonderfully benign power it's like seeing a display of affection between dolphins and – like one's relationship with the warmth that I just mentioned – you instantly fall in love with this pulsing beauty, this extraordinary exhibition of what looks like inter-planetary humanity. There is no option but for me to turn Lumley right there and then.

As a result of a slight misunderstanding with the local tour company, only Roger the cameraman and I have been able to stay out with the Sirius boys. All the rest of the crew, not having sufficient tents or equipment, have disappeared on skidoos back to 'Pointstable' (as our base camp has for some reason become known). Our tent has been rather cunningly lit up with the battery-powered 'ice lights' that Rog uses for subtle ambience (there's not really any situation in life for which the resourceful cameraman isn't perfectly provisioned and skilled). We crawl in and squirm our way into the two sleeping bags the tour people generously remembered to provide. They are thick and warm certainly, but very curiously they have their stiff mattress component built into the bag, which means that if you want to turn in the night (and boy do you want to turn in the night – there's no position that is comfy for longer than twenty minutes at most) the bag won't turn with you, so you have to inch round like a hot-dog sausage turning in its bun.

I notice with envy the next morning that the Sirius guys not only have a thick rubberized mat as a tent-base (vital to keep body heat from seeping out into the permafrost), they also have nifty little blow-up mattresses. After the night I've spent (fully twenty minutes of it in something remarkably close to sleep), I don't think I'd want to sign up for the full twenty-six months. Certainly not in our tent.

It's interesting how your relationship with snow changes at these low temperatures. At home the likelihood is that snow will imminently become water and be a bore. Here it's a good twenty-five degrees away from being wet, so you get quite used to not really worrying about it; it's just a benign sort of dust that clusters around you. It just is everywhere, like fluff. It gathers in the footwells of cars, or in any pocket that hasn't been zipped up, and there it sits, drily, coldly and permanently, never melting, never going anywhere. So when you find it all over the floor of your tent and over your sleeping bag you just leave it. For as long as it doesn't melt – and how would it? – it's not doing any harm.

Something else extraordinary happens overnight, though, because on waking up the next morning I am suddenly forty-five. I have marked the passing of my anniversary on the Arctic ice with the sky music of aurora borealis signalling something or other – I'm not sure what. The toughest night of the trip so far is now behind me and there is compelling euphoria building up inside me: I have survived! We emerge from our tents like all pre-breakfast campers and relish the new day and the prospect of coffee.

The other two of our crew and the guides reappear in our little valley shortly after nine. In less than a minute the Sirius tent is packed and all their kit stowed away on their sled, the huskies are tethered, the boys are in their skis. '*Hunde clar!*' they shout and, like Father Christmas swooshing off to another chimney, they dart away in a cavalcade. All that remains of camp is the tight little formation of frozen husky poos that marks the overnight stopover of thirteen dogs sleeping on the frozen tundra.

10

If the Ice Cap Fits . . . Beard Icicles in Ilulissat

We arrive back at Pointstable, and the sheer luxury of the place, with its warmth and its permanent structure, is overwhelming after the previous night's experience. The need to return to a warm base in these conditions is paramount; the knowledge, when we were out yesterday, that we didn't have any guarantee of comfort at sundown was distinctly unsettling and it is only now, seeing the −1 star Hilton, that we understand quite how much our mental stability has been underwritten by shelter and heat. For the whole following day I wallow in it and savour every kilojoule of the stuff.

I notice that Pointstable, like a number of other places we've been (not least the Icelandic capital, Reykjavik), has permanent Christmas decorations up (much like Oxford Street, come to think of it . . .). There is a Christmas tree made of lights with a big star on the top of it that I haven't really noticed before, or if I have I've just waved it through. It does actually feel Christmassy here – how can it not? The snow is a wonderful thing for putting you in that frame of mind where every act feels like an act of winter goodwill – even going shopping in Reykjavik for family presents felt like Christmas shopping (and the fact that I bought them all thick hairy Skandi-jumpers with snow-flake patterns on, thus prompting biblical outpourings of dismay from at least two of my children, just served to complete the illusion). In fact, given the way my mind works, I wouldn't be at all surprised if much of this trip gets filed in my memories under 'Christmas' simply because of the associations.

Our flight out of Pointstable is scheduled for after lunch the following day. There have been no flights into or out of the base since we arrived, and suddenly the prospect of a flying machine landing here out of a lowering sky seems frankly absurd. The fact that nearly fifty per cent of flights into and out of Constable Point are delayed or cancelled due to its tricky location and somewhat ad hoc facilities just adds to my certainty that it is going to be our home for days and days. If the Tuesday flight is cancelled due to bad weather, we are told, there is no knowing when it will be rescheduled.

When the next day comes, I watch the skies like a war-child all morning. Our flight is delayed, but we're told it is definitely now en route to us. Bang on its new schedule, a very smart Dash 7 lands on our Torvill and Dean runway. We are getting out of here! It's not quite the last 'copter out of Saigon, but it does feel a bit that way.

The plane itself is wonderful and better still it's all ours. We've chartered it because, short of sticking feathers to our arms with wax, it's our only way out of Constable Point. I will love Dash 7s till the end of time just for the memory of our three-hour flight to Ilulissat, 1,000 kilometres almost directly across the country, on the west coast. Not only can we sit anywhere we want in the fifty-odd seats, we even have our very own stewardess – just for the four of us. Better still, there is also a pilot (they come with all the kit!) – an Irishman called Bill who has lived in Greenland for so long his Irish burr has picked up a few chilly intonations of the North. But once we've truffled out the Irish in there, he obligingly ups the burr five or six clicks, even throwing in a couple of 'achs' and a 'sure', which is above and beyond the call.

Below us as we fly due west is the Greenland Ice Sheet. I've taken my eyes off the ground for a moment as the stewardess (our stewardess!) has offered me a cup of tea (cup of tea! It's just like a real aeroplane!), so don't really witness it starting. These things happen – even the most vigilant and conscientious of professional observers will get blindsided by an untimely beverage every now and again. (I believe Joan Didion once forsook a solar eclipse for a delicious Cup-a-Soup.)

At first I just assume it's a layer of thick cloud below us, because all you can see in every direction is flat white ice – an area the size of a continent. Just plain white, like the top of God's mortuary slab, in places apparently up to three kilometres deep. This is the famous Polar Ice Cap, that phrase that I've bandied about far too many times, considering that I haven't, till this moment, known what the hell it actually was.

I thought the ice cap was probably bits of frozen sea, or those melting icebergs that you see polar bears clinging to forlornly on stickers in hotel bathrooms telling us to reuse our towels. But, no, it's the colossal world of compacted snow that straddles Greenland – that's the ice cap. Once again it's bang up there with the Arctic landscape as described to me by my son Paddy. He got it right after all.

We fly for hour after hour as the ice cap rolls on and on – all the way to the west coast of Greenland, where, spoiler alert, the topography changes and mountains peep out once again. The plane (our plane!) banks, and out of the eternal whiteness appear dots of colour. This is Ilulissat, with every house a different hue: pinks, yellows, blues, reds, greens, vivid and beautiful amid the snowy monochrome of the Arctic palette, gathering around the frozen gash of the ice fjord where it opens into the sea ice. As we fly we see a harbour full of boats firmly wedged into thick ice. We land on the tiny runway of the tiny airport and are met by Adrienne the assistant producer with a hire car that she's cunningly managed to park on the runway. (This chartering business is just fantastic; you can do anything you like. Did I mention we had our own stewardess?)

We drive to the Hotel Arctic, a building that proudly displays its four stars everywhere you look. In fact I am beginning to wonder if it isn't actually called the **** Hotel. I just wonder which of the four-letter words on offer they've gone for – shame they haven't given us a steer with a rogue w or an f. We check in; the rest of the crew into the hotel, me into an aluminium igloo overlooking the frozen bay – not, in the event, for reasons of punishment but because it's one of the ****'s little treats.

The first thing we notice about Ilulissat is the step change in temperature. The still air here is cold, the kind of cold that makes you cough involuntarily when you breathe in. Standing by my funny metal igloo I realize I will have to remove my gloves in order to let myself in, and in those twenty glove-lorn seconds my fingers are hurting cold. This is a windless day as well – what the hell is it going to be like when that extra chill kicks in? The sun is setting. Oh yes, that's the other thing about Ilulissat: it's three hours behind the UK. Up till now we've been in Iceland (same time zone as the UK) and Constable Point (theoretically an hour behind, but it was Constable Point so time was almost irrelevant – what time, for example, is it on Mars?). We've jumped several time zones in just three hours. I suppose as you get closer to the Pole that's exactly what you would do, until presumably you can just stroll around every time zone in the world in two seconds.

Ilulissat and the **** (a name I am steadily warming to) do excellent sunsets, because stretching out to the horizon between you and the sinking sun are icebergs sitting vastly and silently in the frozen brine. In our era of air travel you can find yourself stumbling across the extremes of the globe without really having paid enough attention, so that when you come up against unarguable, visible signs of how exotically far you have strayed, you have to pinch yourself and remember that you're not just peering at them through a screen.

I remember reading in my great-grandfather's diaries about his posting to the Indian Civil Service almost immediately after graduating from university in 1894. He describes the voyage to Calcutta, which took weeks and weeks, and how during that time he was able fully to adjust to his new situation. Not only did the incremental change in temperature and daylight mean that he arrived acclimatized, the sheer length of the journey meant that the ungainly 22-year-old Classics scholar who had boarded at Southampton was able to bound on to the Calcutta quayside, a man fully prepared for his new position in life. Here we have just fallen out of a Dash 7 and Wham! we are suddenly in iceberg country. The moustaches of our cameraman and soundman are hung about with icicles after five minutes in the open air. We seem to have peeled a whole new layer off the Arctic onion and arrived at something that looks and feels truly extreme. I mean, we've got bergs and beard-icles, what else do you want?

Ilulissat – formerly Jacobshaven – is a small town of just under 5,000 people (which still makes it the 'third-largest city' in Greenland) and was once the home of Knud Rasmussen, a turn-of-the-century (the last one, not this one) polar explorer who was the first European to cross the Northwest Passage by dog sled. It's located at the end of the Kangia Icefjord which runs down from the Sermeq Kujalleq glacier. Sermeq Kujalleq is the fastest moving glacier in the world. It pings along at 40 metres a day. It used to amble along at a more stately 20 metres daily but seems to have upped its speed in the last ten years.

It's generally supposed that this is due to global warming, which seems a pretty fair guess to me, but precisely how that has sped it up remains a matter of conjecture. The normal rapidity of its progress (because let's face it, 20 metres a day is in itself a world-beating speed for a glacier) is determined by the shape of the valley down which it flows; a huge area of glacial drainage is fed through a relatively small opening on a steep gradient, and so it was never going to be hanging around. The recent increase in its speed could be because the ice cap itself is calving – feeding chunks into the glacier – at a greater rate, thus forcing an increase, or it could be because there is now more meltwater underneath the ice and this lessens the friction that previously restrained it, which in turn could encourage the ice cap to calve more quickly, but no one is entirely certain. As with so many of these indicators of global warming, we are flying blind because we don't have scientifically detailed precedents on record. Therefore to establish cause and effect and to predict future data we have to rely on the conjecture of specialists. And there's the problem.

There are a great many eminent people who are quite

certain global warming is caused by human activity and that we are barrelling towards catastrophe. Given our record of wiping out fish stocks and countless other natural habitats, that would seem to be a plausible and fitting moral end to the story of mankind's greed. But there is also a smaller number of perfectly eminent people who are less convinced and take the view that the earth has natural cycles of hot and cold that generally level out in the end so we shouldn't worry especially, and there's precious little we can do about it anyway.

There is certainly ample evidence of the earth going through a period of warming in recent decades up here in the Arctic, where glaciers have been retreating and sea ice has not been forming where once it did (although this year in Svalbard, Kim the yellow-nosed marksman and 'Side-Saddle' Pilditch both pointed out sea ice in bays where it hadn't been last year – which of course proves nothing other than the unpredictability of local climate variation but rather flies in the face of one climate expert's opinion that there would be no sea ice by 2016), but I have no idea what is a part of the earth's natural ebb and flow and what is a cataclysmic End of Days scenario. The truth is the subject is so huge that you could select data to back up almost any claim (and there have been occasions when data has famously been shown to have been manipulated).

One thing I am allergic to, though, is being told what my opinion on finely balanced specialist debates should be by a mob that wouldn't know the nicer arguments on either side if they sprang out at them from behind a shed. I am genuinely agnostic, therefore, as I find myself agreeing with the last thing I am told by any sensible person on either side of the argument. I believe passionately in sustainability and in eliminating waste, so any improvement on that score made in climate change's name is all splendid by me, but I'm afraid if you are looking for global warming tub-thumping in this diary you will be disappointed. In the interests of impartiality I must report that Siggi, the man behind the ice cave, was convinced there would be no more glaciers in 150 years' time, but in the interests of impartiality I must report that Siggi, the man behind the ice cave, is the man behind the Ice Cave.

After checking in to the ****, we go out for a belated birthday dinner at Ilulissat's number-one eatery (Trip Advisor has been most helpful out here . . .). The restaurant is completely empty all night but for us, and we are waited on, sommeliered and entertained by the chef, who runs the whole show on his own. Shame he didn't strap on a couple of cymbals and a harmonica, as some music would also have been nice. Reindeer has been quite a staple for us since arriving in the Arctic, and after several days of Cross Benny Yeltsin's stodgy Pointstable fare we're all quite pleased to see it back on the menu in this cosy restaurant (sorry, Father C). The night fades into a rosy, vinous blur that feels like a welcome return to civilization.

We are brought shockingly back to our senses, however, when the chef-waiter-barman produces five glasses of the local liqueur after pudding. What is it? We long to know:

'Ah, it's a grouse vodka.' We imagine he must have mistranslated; after all, no one makes vodka out of an animal. He must have meant grape vodka or cloudberry vodka or something like – EURGHHHHACHHHH. Shit no, he really meant grouse vodka, that strange suspension in the liquid must be . . . I dunno, ground-up grouse? Surely not. What the . . .? Why the . . .? GROUSE liqueur?? Why would you DO that? What's wrong with sloe gin? Or just some cognac? Eh? Vodka flavoured with bits of game bird is just yeuch. And when I awake the next morning all I can think about is grouse vodka. All I can taste is grouse vodka. Now I love vodka, and I love grouse, but the cheesy peas principle doesn't really pay off this time.

Our first task today is to do a little research at Silva's shop, Tourist Nature. Silva is a very loud and eccentric Italian who dishes out proper Arctic clothing and high-decibel drollery to travellers while they try to reconcile themselves to the grouse vodka of the night before. We have brought with us layer upon layer of merino wool thermals, fleece shirts, thick fleece zip-ups and massive thick outer coats. This is what ex-Major in the Marines Paul Mattin has selected for us and so far it has served us pretty well, so we decide to bat on with what we have. However, we definitely need better boots – the ones we've brought with us call themselves Comfort –40. Silva explains that what we really need is the Comfort –70 model. Yup, that's right, we need our feet protected against temperatures that are most of the way towards –100. Gah!

* * *

We manage to get ourselves a chopper ride up the ice fjord that afternoon to look at the Sermeq Kujalleq glacier as it whizzes past us. The flight up only takes twenty-four minutes, but we step out, having landed on the glacier, on to the surface of a different planet. Up ahead of us is the ice cap itself, towering like an ice Dover, only with a cliff face that runs for miles and miles.

The glacier that drains this mighty mass takes many different forms and textures; there is one part that looks like the waves of a boiling sea frozen in time, another field has fingers of ice pointing up in square stacks 50 feet tall, another still has swells of ice split by terrifying crevasses 100 feet deep and more. All around are huge round stones that have been picked up by the glacier only to be unceremoniously dumped like a Harry Styles girlfriend. These just serve to add to the lunar-surface effect. The most surprising thing, though, is the colour. The air bubbles trapped in the densely packed ice hold and refract the light as it passes through, so staggering tones of tooth-paste blue and verdigris and even rich dark navy shine like wet limescale in the sunlight on the sheer surfaces of the cliffs.

We step carefully through the snow-topped ice – this is not the place to disappear into a crack. The helicopter pilots obligingly take off for us and fly around so we can film them, and for the first time we're shown how perspective-defyingly huge the whole thing is. Gigantic cliff faces that the eye has told you are nearby turn out to be miles away and therefore six or seven times the already gargantuan size you have thought them. We watch the helicopter as it eventually returns, all of us crossing our fingers. This is the kind of landscape whose lethal beauty and hostility you can only truly appreciate once you are safely out of it. If we were to get 'benighted' here, we'd be done for.

We fly back (thankfully) with Rog the cameraman leaning out of the side door in a harness. The footage he gets is astonishing. Watching it back afterwards you see all the beauty of it, but the innate 'safety' of filmed material filters out the awesome sense of power and threat we felt first hand. This is without question the most overwhelming landscape I have been in in my life. It's impossible to be in such surroundings without your brain becoming involved in it. The swirl and torment of so much terrifying energy held in scarcely credible restraint is something you simply can't look at passively. It's as if a nuclear explosion has been freeze-framed one second after detonation and we are wandering around the spikes of it.

The other big adventure of our time in Ilulissat is to be a dog-sled expedition to Rodebay, an Inuit settlement about 22 km away over the frozen ice. My ticket to Rode (sorry) comes with a very necessary bonus – a lesson in dog sledding from a taciturn fellow called Ono. Ono will be providing the transport to Rodebay and speaks very little English (like most people here he looks at you in under-standable puzzlement if you try to make yourself understood in the usual way, i.e. speaking loudly as if to a halfwit – it actually makes a nice change from the norm to come somewhere so resolutely non-Anglophone). Happily Ono has a wife called Caro: an altogether wonderful person among whose many attributes are an excellent command of English and a sturdy sense of humour.

Caro is one of life's natural aristocrats. She and Ono met while travelling – she was a national cross-country skier in her time – and together they have crossed the ice cap from west to east (forty-eight days of hard going), sledded up to the north of Greenland and across the sea ice to Canada. It's a strange thought that you can get to mainland America on foot from here.

Ono's sled set-up is a million miles away from the Sirius Patrol. To start with, his dogs are a scrappy-looking bunch, covered in scratches and blood and, he tells me as I am harnessing my fifth dog, 'Will bite you.' The Sirius dogs were bred to be much better natured; they would snarl at each other and get into scraps (in fact the one thing Tobias and Caspar worried about if the dogs ever ran off without them was that the dogs would probably kill each other), but they are beautiful, well-kept animals and not remotely aggressive to humans. Ono's gang, by contrast, look mangy and mutinous, and they smell none too savoury to boot. My gloves will hold the musky hum of Ono hound for days. (Well, that's my story and I'm sticking to it.)

The deal with sledding (non-Sirius style) is that you sit on the sled instead of skiing beside it, and when you're good and ready and are sitting comfortably you lean forward and whip away the string that anchors you to your mooring in the snow. Then whoosh! Away you go at a right old lick. The dogs can do almost 40 kmh when they first set off. This eventually slows to walking pace as their initial exuberance dulls, but that is where the true skill of the seasoned driver kicks in.

At any slackening of pace you stir yourself and shout, 'Tuk tuk tuk tuk!' until the dogs – grudgingly – beef it up a little. If you want to go to the left, you shout, '*Venstra venstra!*' If you want to go right, you shout, '*Hoyo hoyo hoyo!*' And if you want the dogs to stop, you sling the old knotted rope around one of the runners and whistle like a tit (a willow tit). As you can see, it's an exceedingly taxing business – some of those words are a nightmare to get your tongue around. Ono has lashed a child's mattress to the sled (which has been built out of old bits of kitchen cabinets, now I look a bit closer) and a couple of reindeer skins ('*Kumfut!*' he shouts, and I am duly grateful).

We head out on to the sea ice and hurtle over the lumps and bumps. Rog has put little GoPro cameras on the front and back of the sled to film my lesson, but the cable ties he tried to use were so cold that the plastic snapped every time it was bent, so instead he just wound them up with gaffer tape. That too froze and lost its stickiness, so after the third time we've gone airborne I am left whistling like a tit and scrabbling around in our icy wake for the missing camera. It isn't just the camera kit that is feeling the cold. By the time I get back to Ono's dog borstal, I am frozen to the marrow. This new level of cold has the efficient brutality of a hungry polar bear, and my polite layers of merino wool just aren't any match for it. Ono tells me that I need better clothes; in fact he says he won't let me sled out to Rodebay unless I have the proper kit. Luckily the fragrant (not in an Ono hound way) Caro has a friend who can sort me out with some sealskins, so we make an appointment to see Agatta the seamstress.

Sealskins are what all the Inuits wear – apart from the odd few I've seen in polar-bear trousers – as nothing comes close to them for warmth. I am measured up for an anorak and trousers, gloves and a new hat and, once decked out in my new Arctic threads, feel my transformation into explorer is complete. Slightly wish I'd gone for a beard, though, so I too could go the full breath stalactite, but there we are.

The next day's sled ride to Rodebay is utterly brilliant: exhilarating, stirring and, of course, extremely physically demanding. Being alone on the sled with just the dogs ahead and the glide of the runners brings home what a hilarious means of getting about this is. Before going any-where, your first job is to harness each of the malodorous and foul-tempered curs that are going to pull you, essentially building your engine, as if you were assembling your horsepower horse by horse.

The dogs all 'Smike' away from you as you approach – their treatment at human hands possibly hasn't been the best – but there are no roads out of Ilulissat, so if you want to travel, you go by dog sled or by boat. The sea ice here is sturdy enough to carry sled traffic nine or ten months of the year, and it's so solid it's almost impossible to tell what is land and what strictly speaking is sea. The sled tracks are evidently well trodden, as the team in front of me needs no further prompting beyond their own training and instincts, so I can just sit back and observe them. I observe that the team pulls in one direction but the individual dogs buzz about, some pulling out to the left then coming back in as others then pull out to the right, like a doggy Newton's Cradle. But there is always some kind of consensus – it's a perfect demonstration of pack mentality. And I observe that one of Ono's dogs has the most monstrous diarrhoea and squirts a pencil-thin hot steady stream most of the way, quite a lot of which clings in frozen globules to its hindquarters just a couple of feet in front of me, bouncing up and down like shiny jewels on the fur.

Generally the lead dog (who has been chosen for her seniority and given an extra foot or two on the length of her tether) will determine the direction of travel, but others can also have an input, particularly if two or three of them decide to alter the course. Bafflingly they do actually follow my calls and turn either to the *Venstra* or *Hoyo* as requested. In truth my job is embarrassingly simple, apart from the bit where I have to stand on the doormat that is nailed to the back of the sled to slow it when going down hill. Ono was showing me how to stand on it when, without warning, he sent the dogs off at full paw and me flying off the back, which I suppose will teach me to hold on in future.

Ono and Caro have a camp halfway, where he suggests we stop in order to warm up – very wise and necessary in the event. We have been going for about two hours when suddenly the lead dog takes a sharp right and we pelt over the sea ice to a huddle of three or four cottages on what must be the 'shore'. Negotiating our way over the edge of the ice is tricky – it is thick and sturdy even 20 feet out, but as you get to the very edge, where there is the most water movement I guess, the ice hasn't settled enough in any one place to form a trusty crust; there are thinner bits and softer bits, where it is wetter and slushier.

We inch our way on foot up to a blue hut for which Caro produces a key. There's an outdoor porch with various bits of fishing equipment in it and scary dried fish hanging and spinning like the world's biggest most eccentrically scented magic trees, which must mean that in summer this bay unfreezes and quite possibly becomes rather lovely. In winter, though, it is very much just a hut on the edge of the icy wastes that serves as a handy bothy for freezing travellers and not much else. But what a hut! The main part, once an inner door has been unlocked, is strikingly modern: a large single room with a double bunk bed and a kitchenette with a plain, neat laminated floor and a stove that keeps it warm all the time. There are windows on three sides looking out and a table with four chairs.

This would actually be a wonderful benightment. There is a wind turbine behind and solar panels too, so there's no shortage of power. You could hole up here and be incredibly cosy and self-sufficient. I should think the bird life on the water in front would be an endless source of entertainment in the warmer months. I do notice there are strange transparent orbs strung up like Christmas baubles along the ceiling, each about two inches in diameter and with something that looks remarkably like black maggots nestling in the bottom. I ask what these might be. 'Grouse stomachs,' comes the reply. 'We take them out and dry them – they're a Greenlandic delicacy.'

Yes, those little black maggots just visible through the transparent gut lining globes look remarkably like what was floating in our post-prandials the other night. I try to find out more about this local speciality at a later point, but it's not especially well documented, although I do discover that Inuits would historically catch grouse and ptarmigan and eat their intestines before selling the rest of the carcass to more (or less, depending on your point of view) discerning eaters. This was where they found their essential vitamin C to keep from getting scurvy – the curse of so many Arctic exploration parties over the centuries. Oh Lord, just as I've managed to forget the grouse-y stickies we threw down our necks a few nights before, here they are crowding back into my mind and tastebuds and repeating.

Sitting on my little children's mattress (which, as Ono promised, is the last word in kumfut) and pegging it along to Rodebay after our little halfway stop, I worry for the first time about frostnip (the first phase of frostbite). Paul Mattin (who's an ex-Major in the Marines, you know, and has spent more months in the Arctic than I've had hot drinks with him in various meeting rooms) warned us that the skin over our cheekbones was particularly susceptible and sure enough that is where I'm feeling the cold start to dig in. I find that by holding my gloved hand up there and by moving my cheeks up and down by pulling big V for Vendetta smiles every five seconds I can keep it at bay. The glove is so heavily impregnated now with the fine musk of Ono's dogs, though, that this brings certain other problems of its own.

There's something enormously pleasing about the dog sled as a means of transport. It's not fast, obviously, but then it doesn't need to be, as no one's routinely travelling great distances and, even if they are, it's part of the Inuit way to do it slowly and to absorb every detail of the journey. But best of all it's completely free. The dogs will eat pretty much anything and are fed on a family's kitchen leftovers (skin, bone, scraps, etc.), which means that transport in this part of Greenland is almost entirely fuelled by waste. And that, apart from when it disagrees with the dogs, as it quite vehemently does with one of mine today, is just tremendously satisfying.

11

Seal Meat Again . . .

Rodebay is a tiny settlement of forty-three people. We are staying in the 'town's' 'hotel', the Nordlys, which is run by Ole, the mayor of Ilulissat. He has very decently given up his weekend to come and look after us. The hotel is still kind of being built, though. There are bits of timber and rawl plugs lying around and a huge box with a flat screen telly in it waiting to be unpacked and screwed to the wall. But it is warm and we are evidently the only guests. Ole brings through a steaming pot of soup for us and puts some frozen pizzas in the oven. It seems idiotic to bang on endlessly about the cold – this is the Arctic after all – but this is a particularly cold moment. Our arrival at the Nordlys is followed by about half an hour's silent absorption of warmth. And – no less importantly – pizza.

I perhaps should have gone a little easier on the latter as I've got an appointment with an Inuit couple only two hours later that, inevitably, involves being asked to sit down and have supper with them (or whatever it is you eat at 4 p.m. Tea?). Amalia and Mattias don't speak a word of English but are delightful. Amalia has a touch of steel about her (as you'd need living up here), meanwhile, Mattias just nods and smiles the kindest, crinkliest smile you've ever seen. Their house is roasting hot – maybe in our honour – and a splendidly welcoming place, the walls covered with pictures of children and grandchildren in traditional Inuit costume. I am shown straight through to the kitchen and presented with a bowl of seal soup and a few odds and sods of seal bones with meat attached – one that you might call a chop, the other a bit of lower vertebra like you'd find in an Irish stew. It's not bad, seal meat; it has the texture of school-cooked liver and something about its taste that reminds me of lamb. If I hadn't been quite so greedy with Ole's soup 'n' pizza earlier, I'd have probably been able to eat loads.

Happily Caro is on hand to translate Amalia's soft, throaty Greenlandic. Seal hunting is something that Inuit couples do together, she says. Amalia herself takes the 'traditional role' of shooting the seal, which strikes me as a surprising division of labour (before I immediately berate myself for imposing gender stereotypes ...). But that's what is so refreshing here: the business of survival is a family endeavour; there has clearly never been any sense of the li'l lady staying at home while the men go off to hunt and gather, perhaps because, as generations of polar explorers learnt, if you sit around doing nothing in this climate you tend to die.

Now I come to think about it, in the admittedly few Inuit families I've come across, the husband and wife seem to work very much as a team. I wonder if this admirable scenario is the norm in Greenland, and I wonder too if it comes from their more evenly shared traditional roles. Once Mattias is presented with the seal, he is then in charge of skinning it and treating the pelt. Together they butcher the carcass for freezing and all the leftovers are kept for feeding the dogs. There is not a single molecule of the seal that isn't put to use. This is, as we've come to expect from these northern peoples, full and respectful use of the animal they kill to survive.

The season for hunting seals is the summer, so, strangely, the Inuits need deep freezes (I'd imagined they'd just use an outdoor cupboard, which would surely do the trick . . . but in the summer the temperature is often above freezing). Amalia produces a tool whose shape we have seen everywhere since arriving in Greenland: it has a T handle and a round mezzaluna blade. This is the ulu, the traditional tool for skinning seals, which has become the national symbol of Greenland. It all makes perfect sense; ex-Major in the Marines Paul Mattin taught us that food, shelter and warmth are the things that will keep us alive in Arctic conditions, and this tool has provided the indigenous people of the perishing Pole with all three of those things. It is the symbol of the Inuits' extraordinary triumph in the face of the most unlikely odds. For centuries – long before heating in homes was provided by gas or oil – they have thrived at these ludicrous temperatures thanks to the seals they live off. Do they have a quota on the number of seals they take in the season? 'No,' replies Amalia, 'we just take what we need.' Amalia and Mattias don't have space for any more seal meat than they can eat over a winter, and so they know exactly what provisioning they require.

Many people for some reason object to the killing of seals by the Inuit people – at first I too couldn't quite shake off the inherent unease it provoked, probably because of the stories of seal clubbing in Canada in the sixties and seventies and the way commercial sealing over there had brought the population of harp seals down to vanishingly low numbers. But again, you see, that's commercial food production for you. It's always the mindless mercantile element that brings in all the very worst, inhumane practices: the ruin of natural habitats and decimation of perfectly balanced animal populations that have sustained us and themselves for millennia.

How Amalia and Mattias hunt is a world away from the mass slaughter of the commercial sealers. Like Børge with his Lofoten cod, their prey is taken and killed individually. There is something tidier and more grimly clinical about the mechanized commercial mass slaughter of animals – it happens out of sight, so we can generally ignore it, and we'll cheerfully buy our neatly packaged, politely shaped supermarket meat without a care for its backstory – which causes us to look on those who kill individual wild animals to eat as the bloodthirsty savages. But in truth there is something a good deal more honest – and infinitely more sustainable and environmentally friendly – about how they procure their food. The seal is at the heart of Amalia's and Mattias's culture as well as at the heart of their family's survival – it has almost religious connotations for them; they revere it as well as depend on it. I hope that people who object will try to see it in that light and maybe understand it a bit better.

I've eaten as much in the last four hours as a prudent Inuit family might in a week, so it's a good job I have a bit of activity lined up for the evening. Tonight I am going to join the Rodebay Club for their Friday hooley. Polka dancing came over to Greenland with the European trappers and whalers of the nineteenth century and has taken firm root. I make my way over to the church hall and am greeted by the sight of more colour than I have seen for days – the traditional costumes are out in full and dazzling array: white sealskin boots with embroidered trim and fur at the top; a white anorak jumper, again trimmed with fox fur; and a beaded bib that runs right over the shoulders, back and front, decorated with bright coloured patterns.

I've seen this costume before and, like many other national costumes, it's rather garish and weird taken out of context, but up here it looks utterly fabulous. There's so little colour around in general that my eyes drink in the gaudy shades gratefully and indiscriminately like it's the beautiful random splurge of a June flowerbed – it is genuinely uplifting to see. The beads, I learn, are tiny coloured pearls; heavy great thunks of mineral (or animal – what actually is a pearl? Somewhere between the two, I guess) that must make a simple polka feel like hoofing around under jockey's weights. That explains the finely turned calves of all these Rodebayans . . .

I am provided with some traditional clothes of my own, as Bertholine, my partner for the night (an absolutely heavenly smiley lady about a foot and a half shorter than me, who turns out to be Mattias's sister), takes one look at my cold-weather gear and tuts – it clearly won't do. (Had I but known, I'd have packed some dancing pumps and tails . . .) A pair of loose black trousers, some black Cornish-pasty slip-ons and a white anorak top are swiftly handed over, and I am ushered into the black-bag loos of the village hall, where I slip into my dancing togs under the watchful teeth of beaming teenagers on a series of Greenlandic anti-smoking posters. I emerge looking like the last supply dentist on the books of a condemned agency.

Bertholine evidently believes in throwing you (or, in this case, me) in at the deep end. There is to be no demonstration of the basic polka moves; I am simply going to have to follow the pair in front and do my best. Bertholine giggles throughout, which is nice of her – she could easily have tutted and seethed at my ineptitude, it's her Friday night's toes I am stepping on, after all. I botch my way through it with the spurts and halts of someone singing an unknown hymn. By the time the band on the CD have reached the long chord that signals 'end', I am baking hot, quietly confident that I've got the hang of it and itching to do more.

I can see how the polka has stuck around for so long. It's like dancing reels: you can't initially imagine yourself doing it or indeed anything more humiliating, until you actually join in and surprise yourself with how much fun it is. It's a straightforward way of passing time and keeping yourself warm. And there is plenty of time up here in the winter months, certainly when the days are short (if they choose to happen at all), and keeping active, getting up and finding yourself tasks to do is – as I mentioned – a key part of survival: you snooze, you lose (the will to live). It took polar explorers until the eighteenth century to twig that the parties that went out hunting, or building cabins, or exploring on sleds were the ones that stayed mentally and physically healthy. Anyone who slipped into indolence and lassitude quickly went under. Indolence and lassitude aren't in Bertholine's vocabulary (although to be fair neither are words like 'thank you', 'goodnight' and 'I'm so sorry, I hope your toes are all right', but I hope she got the message all the same).

We trip and slide our way back to the Nordlys, glowing like red-hot polkas and exuding well-being for at least 30 feet of the journey before the heat dissipates. The mayor of Ilulissat (who has also been at the polka dancing) has somehow managed to cook up a supper of garlicky Greenlandic prawns, then roast lamb and dauphinoise potatoes. His wife talked him through the recipes over the telephone, he says. She can be proud of what he's achieved: that dauphinoise is a monument to the humble tuber. At one point as I go to fill the water jug – a rare moment on this particular night, as pretty much every other drop we drink is either wine or whisky – the mayor points me to a blue plastic drum in the corner: 'Dip the jug there,' he instructs.

Unsure if we've understood each other correctly, I nevertheless take off the heavy blue lid. Inside are several gallons of clear water with huge chunks of ice bobbing around, so I fill the jug as instructed, half-expecting him to burst out laughing at some joke, the funny side of which we will all eventually see . . . But, no, this is absolutely the right course of action. The drum is full of meltwater – like a more domesticated version of what we drank on the Sirius. I only hope Ole doesn't gather his snow too close to the house, as we have taken the view that it would be wasteful to fill his heavy-duty black bag with liquid, especially when we can have such fun making yellow holes in the snow outside (I am aware that this will come as a smack in the face to ex-Major in the Marines Paul Mattin after all his exhortations to keep extremities covered, but given how perfectly safe it turned out to be, you've got to ask yourself what the guy in his picture must have done to earn himself such a black mark – and I use the words advisedly). And as the night wears on and gets later and colder and we become strangely lazier, our journeys out from the back door get shorter and shorter . . .

The following morning I come into the mayoral kitchenette to ask if I can make some tea. Ole looks up from his drying-up, seemingly less than delighted. 'Tea?' he asks. 'Tea,' I confirm, only a bit louder this time to be helpful. Ole doesn't like the sound of this one bit. 'TEA?' Yes, I insist – or coffee – I point to the kettle and mime drinking. The poor multi-tasked servant of the people rolls his eyes and, having misunderstood my request, says 'May I finish this first, please?' brandishing his drying-up cloth as he does so. I do my best to convey in the language of out-stretched fingers that I didn't mean to put him to any trouble, but I fear the damage is done. All the bonhomie of the night before – the polka dancing, the seal eating, the gallons of wine drinking – has vanished like a shot of grouse vodka down a gullible person's throat.

Word will doubtless spread around the village about our insatiable demands, so remorseless that they've sapped even a senior local government official of his habitual sangfroid. Later, Rog is sending up the heli-camera to take aerial shots of the settlement and takes some stills of the hotel as seen from 300 feet up to send to Ole by way of thanks for his exceptional hospitality, which I hope atones for my unintentional faux pas. Much to my chagrin I have learnt that speaking English slowly and loudly with accompanying hand gestures is not in itself enough to ensure peaceful global relations. I wonder if John Torode has been told . . .

With its flushing loos, roads, shops and bustling populace, Ilulissat feels like a throbbing metropolis on our return. A common sight in Ilulissat, incidentally, is young parents out pushing buggies along the road, taking the (–30°) air. Why this should strike me as remarkable I have no idea – people push buggies everywhere, but there we are. It's something I haven't really seen since we've been at such low temperatures. I suppose there aren't any parks – or at least not in the winter – and so the only walk you can go on with a buggy is along the road. And having no pavements – as they don't – means you take more notice of pedestrians as you swerve to avoid them. Maybe the buggies are empty and it's a way of ensuring more careful swerving from the drivers. Maybe it's a useful handle to have in front of you on a slippery surface – acting a bit like a Zimmer frame. Or, hell, maybe it just shows that there's a healthy number of young families staying put in Ilulissat rather than heading off to the bright lights of Nuuk (Greenland's capital). Who knows, but isn't that remarkable, eh? Young parents pushing buggies. Whatever next?

The next day is a Sunday, and just in case we have overlooked this fact the **** for once stops playing Elton John on its in-house sound system (hilariously, *Too Low For Zero* is the core of their playlist, not only climatically apt but also packed with much-loved forgettable hits from my early teens), replacing Elton with congregational Lutheran hymns all morning. Having spent many hundreds of my life's Sunday mornings chugging through hymns ancient and modern, splendid and dire, I find it oddly comforting. Slightly strange to broadcast it to the entire building on

Grappling with Eva – the action shots were actually too disturbing for a family audience.

Journey to the glacier.

Could the last one back in the tent turn out the spectacular Northern Lights?

On the Icelandic tectonic ridge.

Ice harvesting from above, where Jens Olla's sarcasm is not discernible.

Hotel pod, aka 'God's Travel Lodge'.

With David and Jenna ... and not a beaver in sight.

Operating the jackhammer – stitch this, *Top Gear*.

Looking slightly apprehensive about how Denis might've come by these hubcaps.

The Bombardier: Arctic runabout with a difference.

Reformed brothel, Bombay Peggy's.

Because no holiday photo album would be complete without the obligatory 'standing by a sign' shot ...

Hot springs eternal.

As bathrooms go, this one was on the airy side.

Diomede from the reluctant 'copter.

The crew (from l-r): Dom, Rog, Hermione, Self, James and our fixer Shane at the front.

the public address system, maybe, but then I grew up in a household where, at Radio 4's morning junction, we would always go the hymns-and-cricket route of Long Wave – with my parents singing loudly along to the hymns as if it were the most natural thing in the world.

Long Wave has the great advantage of being a kind of split-screen station in that you can usually hear up to fifteen different broadcasts simultaneously on any bandwidth, as if Jonathan Agnew were hunched over a microphone in the middle of a crowded souk while an opera singer and the head of a military junta duke it out in the booth next door (this is almost exactly how I imagine *Test Match Special* to be – listening to it on digital and without all the whistles and bells of AM takes a lot of drama out of it if you ask me). It is funny how tiny little resonances from home, when you're in an environment as desolate as this, can bring enormous comfort.

We've made a provisional plan to go out in a boat to survey the icebergs with a dour man in a beanie hat called Jens Olla. Jens Olla is an ice harvester who supplies our hotel – among others – with all its bar ice. After an early breakfast, we get to the harbour, replete with smoked halibut and Sunday hymns, to find Jens Olla scowling beneath his beanie.

'We'll never get out today.' He is adamant.

Why not?

'Look!' he says, taking in the bay of ice with a sweep of his arm. 'Ice!'

We see his point: there is indeed a lot of ice. Although

this is Greenland, and there doesn't appear to be any more ice than we saw, for example, yesterday, when the slender channel of thinner ice leading out of the bay was choked with vessels of one kind or another.

Jens Olla looks disgusted – disgusted at the cold snap we have apparently had in the hours preceding our voyage, disgusted at the sheer iciness he sees around him, disgusted at our inability to appreciate the dangers of going out in ice. I can't help feeling that, as an ice harvester by trade, he must've come across conditions like this a couple of times before, but it seems that this is too horrific a day for us even to contemplate going out of the harbour. Jens Olla is reduced by the impossibility of the venture to a series of gestures, grunts, spirited forehead rubs and spits: getting out to sea is a total impossibility.

As we bob about in the open sea, Jens Olla's spirits lift. Getting out of the harbour has, it transpires, been a doddle. The repeated ramming of the thinner ice in the channel has been wonderfully satisfying. Occasionally we come across a thicker plate and the bows ride up until – crack! – the crust breaks and we slide on. The ship was built for this job, and it seems to relish the bruising progress it makes, sometimes leaving a daub from its red-painted hull on the ice as a marker.

The hull is made of railway-sleeper-thick thunks of some heavy brute of a wood. Out in the bay, once free from all but the slushiest layers, the icebergs are next on the agenda. These beautiful silent scoops of anciently frozen water, some as big as thirty football fields in length and width and higher than Everest from tip to bottom, are the most extreme symbol of the Poles. Nothing else is as ridiculous as them, nothing as far from our understanding of the temperate world.

Pictures of icebergs cannot prepare you for the scale of the things when they are in front of you; even the tiny fraction (between a sixth and a tenth of the whole) that peeps above the sea towers and stretches into unlikely distances. These land masses of glinting sharp edges and improbable grace only reveal the sheer clip at which they travel out from the fjord when viewed on time-lapse footage. Like the sculptures of the Ice Hotel, these too are temporary structures, but these works of art, heart-breakingly beautiful, will melt unseen, unremarked upon, unknown and unapplauded. I am going to say this now – forgive me if I'm telling you something you've known all your life but this was a new one on me – icebergs are made of fresh water. They are what the flow of ice from the polar ice cap turns into after it gets to the end of the glacier – they break off and float away into the sea. In all likelihood the iceberg that sank the *Titanic* came from the Kangia Icefjord, where we are now floating (that's like being told that Evel Knievel came from your village, isn't it?).

Once Jens Olla has spotted what he's after, we pull up alongside one of the smaller bergs. He gets his tools ready (a bucket and a small kitchen knife), and we hop down on to the even snow that covers up the deeply uneven surface of the berg below it. Has he ever fallen into the sea? 'Oh, yes, many times – ha ha!' (Jens has suddenly become quite chipper, and his heart now appears to be completely in this expedition.) He sweeps some snow off a large chunk of ice and demonstrates the basic method of harvesting.

You stab away at the blue stuff in a *Basic Instinct* kind of a way and, as the tip of your knife touches the ice, there's a deep pop and chunks fly off. Seriously, it's like having cocktails up the Magic Faraway Tree, and every bit as addictive. Every part of the berg is full of tiny bubbles of compressed air – first (remember?) it was snow and then as the weight of each passing year's snowfall built above it, it compressed along with the air inside it, until at the bottom of the glacier the bubbles now contain air that is as old as the dinosaurs and as small as pinpricks. This is the stuff that calves into the sea, and these icebergs are truly exquisite.

Stab – pop – stab – pop – stab – pop – stab – pop. The bucket fills quickly with dry, frozen chunks of ice crystal. We stagger back to the boat under the weight of our bounty, but I could have happily done this all day. Before we can leave, Jens Olla has a vital household chore to perform: he fetches a big blue plastic drum from the wheelhouse – this is his family drinking water and needs to be replenished, so we fill it with the smaller bits of breakage, occasionally Sharon Stoning for a few more choice booms of ice.

This must be how everyone in these parts gets their water (suddenly I realize that Ole's drinking water was from further afield than I'd given it credit for), and it's totally pure, Jens explains, as it has so far had no contact with the earth and therefore has no mineral content.

'There is nothing purer to drink on the planet than this,' he says. 'Put some in your mouth.'

I lift up a piece of crackling berg ice and . . . it bloody sticks to my lip. Oh, how Jens Olla larfs!

Part Three

The Final Frontier:
North American Arctic

12

Yellowknife – Paris of the Yellowknife Area

After seeing a bit of the Northwest Passage from the west coast of Greenland and having been within touching distance (all right, dog-sledding distance) of Canada, it will be no surprise to learn that the land of Bryan Adams, Celine Dion and Rush is to be our next destination. Actually we've cheated a bit, because we start off our Canadian leg 250 miles south of the Arctic Circle in Yellowknife, the largest city in the Northwest Territories. Yellowknife is in the Arctic 'region' at least, if not right up in the Circle, and must qualify even if only by dint of how sodding cold it is. We fly first to Edmonton, then Calgary, both of which are very reasonable and English in temperature, but Yellowknife is a casual –29° when we touch down. The sun glinting off the frozen compacted ice creates the illusion of the most heavenly spring day, but take that first step off the aeroplane and there is no arguing with the knacker cold.

My first impression of Yellowknife is of a different kind of Arctic – it's a much beefier, more First World affair than that we left behind us in ol' Greeners. The cars are bigger and shinier and have Northwest Territories number plates all cutely shaped like polar bears. The cars in Ilulissat were thirty years old, from an era before power steering, airbags, central locking and all that la-la. If they had number plates at all, they were as likely as not swinging by one rusty bolt from the boot. And the snow in the footwells, for all we knew, could have been there since it tumbled from a winklepicker (a thermal winklepicker, obvs) tapping away to Classix Nouveaux.

Car parts in Ilulissat would quite arbitrarily stop working and furtive roving mechanics would have to turn up suddenly where we were filming, fix the buggered door or jammed handbrake and then slip away into the permafrost. Canada's mechanics work in big garages, like Billy Joel in the 'Uptown Girl' video, and eat slices of delivery pizza. Massive slices obviously: we're in North America. But it's just curious to see a different mode of human presence in what is still a bitterly hostile environment. The human settlements in Greenland were tentative affairs where people lived on the land and gingerly went about the business of existence. In Canada, as in the UK, everyone is at the end of a huge supply chain; if sheet ice in October prevents the musk ox from eating the grass and wipes out a couple of million of them, the chicken supplies will still come through to KFC, the shelves in the supermarkets will still warp under the weight of groceries from all over the world.

This way of living is very appealing and familiar to us, but coming to it from Greenland, you see how it breeds a civilization that brooks no argument about its assured place in the world. Nature becomes something we turn to merely for pleasure and comes to us in the form of marvelling at sunsets or building chapels out of ice. There is none of the humility of old Amalia and Mattias quietly eking out their time with seals and polkas. What few bits remain of the 'old' Yellowknife (rows of gnarled and weathered wooden huts) have been put in dread heritage inverted commas to become much-sought-after bijou residences or jewellery shops (bijoux residences) for the new generation of frontiers people who come up here to listen to Vampire Weekend, live in kooky shacks and sell execrable geegaws. It's strange how quickly our bottle-fed modern world loses meaningful contact with its past. We simply don't draw our sustenance from roots any more, and so the world we live in becomes just a location, an X on Google Earth, rather than a fragile habitat with which we take out a binding contract.

So far in Canada I've noticed the following: the loos in both hotel bathrooms barely raise themselves off the floor; man, have you got to crouch to sit on those. In fact the bathrooms (both of the ones I've seen) have turned their back, in a way that I wholly respect, on normal hotel regulations by having light switches and plug sockets in them and even, in my current bathroom, an iron. A sodding IRON in the bathroom. All plugged in and everything, perfect for lobbing into a full bath in case I need to kill a ruthless henchman in a faintly comical way. I have also come across a notable number of Canadian women with HUGE personalities. I mean, wonderful, witty, forthright, warm – all that – but just colossal, strident, often loud characters. Is that a Canadian thing? So far that would be a fair description of, let's say, about 85 per cent of the women I've met since arriving in Canada. It sounds awfully judgemental, but it's not meant to – on the contrary, it's a very easy national trait to warm to, I'm just noting the fact that the ratio is way higher than you would normally come across.

I have also found some Grade A stickling for rules (apart from in the bathroom department). We were kept back at the airport by security and questioned about the camera batteries we all have to carry in our hand luggage. These, it must be said, are impressively sinister-looking things, each the size and weight of a brick but with red and green wires protruding from them and each wrapped up in neoprene (to keep the cold out and extend their use in Arctic conditions) and heavily gaffer-taped, i.e. conforming in every tiny detail to what I would expect a bomb to look like. We have to carry them in our hand luggage because they are apparently apt to burst into flames at normal cargo-hold temperatures. We have waltzed through every airport security section since we left England – admittedly we learnt early on that it was better to 'produce' the batteries (i.e. remove them from our rucksacks) rather than have to watch them being fished out by the staff and weather the shocked looks of our fellow travellers – but here in Canada we were fully interrogated for half an hour and the batteries very nearly impounded. Then, bizarrely and without any warning at all, they suddenly let us go, batteries and all. Maybe they just got bored or had done enough to win the bet. The cabin crew flying us to Yellowknife (female, colossal personalities) marched up and down the aisle upholding to the letter ancient and archaic electronic device rules of yesteryear that have long since been dropped by the more progressive airlines. And yet they put an IRON in a bathroom. An iron.

I have also noticed the static electricity here – hard not to notice it really, as every time you pass anything faintly metallic huge jolts of sparking energy zap through your fingers' ends, often quite painfully, with the consequence that I now catch myself trying to summon lifts by pressing the button with a pen or turning lights on through my jumper – idiocy, obviously, as the spark ALWAYS FINDS YOU IN THE END. Having turned out the light in my hotel room (and been zapped for the trouble), the sheets and pillowcase on my bed crackle with sparky phosphorescence like my own private Northern Lights every time I move. This is kind of cool but has got me worrying. You see, one of the unalloyed joys of being away from the marital bed is the virtuosic breaking of wind to which you can give full and free rein, but I genuinely start to wonder about the wisdom of allowing such a methane build-up when a mini Fifth of November accompanies my every night-time twitch. It's quite possible that I have cracked the riddle of spontaneous human combustion.

Our first day in Yellowknife has me landing in a twin otter with skis on the ominously named Great Slave Lake (in fact named after the Slavey tribe, who used to live here, rather than after an army of subjugated labourers – as far as I can gather the white man's behaviour towards the indigenous peoples was in the main a good deal better this far north than it had been in other territories. His main objective in the Arctic region seems to have been to get through it as quickly as possible in order to reach other territories where he could hold dominion and subjugate the locals).

I don't believe anyone has bothered counting up all the lakes of Canada. It would be a thankless task in the first place and anyone you shared the result with would probably just punch you out of sheer boredom. There are just too many of them, from the tiny to the colossal to those several times the size of Wales (poor Wales – always being used as the device for measuring other countries' lakes). Great Slave Lake is several times the size of Wales and for eight months of the year it has ice on it as thick as a Welshman is tall. For the people of Yellowknife this is a tremendous boon as it means they can drive on the lake (or land aeroplanes with skis on it), and all the coastal areas that are a bore to reach in the summer are just a few minutes' drive away over the Gavin-Henson-thick ice.

Fishermen too can skid about to find choice ice holes where they can ply their trade.

One such, a very sweet man called Shane, meets us from the plane in his Bombardier (a strange yellow-submarine-looking vehicle – he's painted it rather a dashing powder blue to throw us off the scent – on caterpillar tracks) and drives us in to the shore of old Yellowknife. Shane has brought his five-year-old son, KL, with him (I like a child named after a South-East Asian capital . . .). KL generally sits quietly or plays games on his dad's phone, but Shane keeps up an endless stream of questions, pointing at things wide eyed and, before we leave, he asks if we have any stickers for him. Stickers? 'Yeah, you know for sticking maybe on cars? No worries if you don't. Be cool, though, to have some stickers.'

At the edge of the lake sit about two dozen houseboats, at this time of year stolidly wedged up with snow and ice. They're called houseboats, but the boat element is really just a tiny nod to the fact that they're built on floating platforms. What you're essentially looking at is a large shed-type dwelling – not a million miles away from Ono and Caro's pad on the ice track to Rodebay – that bobs. We are here to meet a couple called Monique and Daniel who run a B&B in one of these and who kindly take us in for lunch. We've taken rather longer than expected to get to them, so they set about lunch preparations with gusto.

'My goodness, you must be starving, right on!' – they say this quite a lot – 'Let's get lunch sorted right away. Lunch, lunch, lunch. OK, what kind of tea do you want?

Orange Pekoe? We had a guy from China here who's a tea inspector and he said this was about as good as Orange Pekoe gets. Hope it's OK!'

'Daniel, will you get going with those apple slices – they're hungry.'

In no time lunch is ready and I am sitting down to apple slices – which come with a dip in a bowl (What's this? 'Yoghurt!') and tea. Mmmmm, apple slices with yoghurt dip and Orange Pekoe tea. All that's missing is kumquats with mustard to make it the classic lunch.

Daniel and Monique are hilarious, though. They've both come here to escape Ottawa. I've never been to Ottawa, so I don't know what they were escaping from – maybe a bear had got in – but up here they have found the perfect place to live, a house(boat) with sunlit windows on three sides, a wood-pellet-burning stove that heats the interior bio-dynamically to a balmy 30° while storms of –60 might be blowing outside. Solar panels provide the electricity for their computers ('We don't have a television – we just don't watch it.' What's that screen upstairs? 'That's for DVDs.' 'Yah, we don't even watch documentaries.'). It's a very beguiling lifestyle (apart from the TV bit, of course – that just sounds like madness), and I can easily see why they've fallen in love with it. Being on the lake and watching the seasons unfold while you are warm and self-sufficient inside. It's very cosy. They take in guests, which I hope explains the number of pieces of paper, full of underlined instructions, sticking to various walls.

Daniel and Monique built their houseboat themselves

– and the one next door that serves as Monique's studio. Oh wait! Studio! Of course! That explains the canvas of a naked Daniel holding a cat. And the papier-maché horse with the fish-scale mane leaping out of the wall. Yes, yes, yes. Monique must be an *artist*. She has a character that breaks over you in waves and tells stories accompanied by gales of passionate laughter that give you the sense that Monique in a bad mood is probably something to be avoided. Daniel explains that he is part-English-part-Scottish-part-Dutch, and at that moment I discern a likeness to Van Gogh that I can't quite shake for the rest of the day. As I write this even now I picture Daniel with a bloodied bandage around his head. He seems to have that thing that people on second marriages often have of being very careful to be fair and even-tempered at all times (he and Mon have been together for seven years), but later on when I am helping him pump lake water into their tanks I wonder if I can't hear the muffled cry of a rather more forceful Daniel tightly restrained within this easy-going Yellowknifer. They are lovely people and very generous but do nothing to unburden me of my deep-rooted suspicion that many of those people who make a great song and dance about being free spirits are often the most inflexible people you could possibly wish to meet.

We join a few of Daniel's and Monique's friends for a game of 'Shinny' (this seems to be what they all call ice hockey) on a makeshift rink on the lake. Daniel suggests that I have a skating lesson with him for a few minutes and then play ice hockey with them. This, I have a hunch, is a bad idea. I've seen ice hockey being played by Canadians; it's not something you want to get mixed up in – even if you were born wearing skates. Anyway, I duly complete my obligatory skating lesson and get really very good at hobbling around on the ice with my arse sticking out while holding on to a collapsible chair – the chair being Daniel's teaching aid – much as young beginners at Somerset House learn to skate with small plastic penguins. Happily boredom comes to my rescue and even Daniel's good intentions can't veil his sheer blood-tear-inducing frustration at my ineptitude. I relinquish my skates to Daniel, who puts on a brief show of 'No, no, you're fine' before lacing them up and putting them to altogether better use. Bloody hell these people can play ice hockey. We watch D&M and friends blur as they skim and swerve and pirouette and glide around the rink, scraping tight little turns on the ice – never once falling over – and all the while whacking a puck around from to stick to stick. From time to time they even knock it through one or other of the two tiny little holes in wooden pallets at each end that serve as goals. Obviously if I'd had half an hour more to practise I'd be right there with them . . .

We file off from the lake to find supper at Bullocks Bistro, a place that has the delightful knack of sounding like bollocks whenever Canadians say it. Bullocks is extraordinary, and I'm pleased to say it earns every single syllable of the guff we've heard about it since arriving in Canada (a very spirited lady next to me on the plane from Calgary made me promise we'd come here). It's run – and this'll surprise you – by two 'larger than life' women who cook everything behind an enormous counter covered in saucy bumper stickers and swooning diners' graffiti and ignore you. They are hilarious in that 'local colour' way one rather longs for in a town with too many laminated menus. We aren't in any hurry so sit happily at the counter/bar for the half-hour or so before someone – with great reluctance – takes our orders. Most things that are on the menu have either run out or are not in season. But this is suddenly rather charming, and it feels for the first time that we might actually be somewhere that is on speaking terms with the wilds outside. Food is piled high on to massive trenchers. For most of the waiting time we watch as about 10lb of salmon steaks are spiked on to a kebab – this is one person's Fisherman's Platter. Every time we go to a restaurant here I feel like I'm hiding in a giant's kitchen. If I really were needing to pile into 9,000 calories a day, this would be pretty much a one-stop shop.

The next morning Dom, Rog, James (the new soundman who's been with us since Iceland), Hermione (who's back with us for the last leg) and I are chartering a flight from Yellowknife up to Dawson City in the Yukon and have instructions to present ourselves at the Buffalo Airways terminal at the airport. Buffalo, we discover, are quite the local celebs as they've featured in six seasons' worth of *Ice Pilots*, a show on Canada's History Channel. This, one presumes, is why we have to be ushered around the place by Pete, a substantial man who could give a plate of lightly cooked mince a good run-in in any IQ contest. I'm not entirely sure he understands what our relatively straight-forward requirements are (go in, film a piece to camera beside some old DC3s and DC4s that are part of the Buffalo fleet, film a plane taking off, load up, take off, fly to Dawson), but he makes the heaviest weather of it. We are lectured – five responsible adults – by Pete – big meaty man, shouty voice – on the dangers of a working airfield. We are to stick together at all times – 'Any one of you runs off like a dog after a squirrel then we're all back in here and it's off. Y'understand? Right, now let's get out there and have the heck some fun.' (I promise he said that.)

We stick rigidly to Pete's dictum while he ties himself up in knots. 'You two go and bring the car round, I'll go to my office and . . .' But shouldn't we all stick together? 'Yup, you're right! Let's all go and get the car.' But we won't all fit into it. 'OK, you all wait here.' He disappears for a few minutes then comes back. 'I must apologize for earlier, we've had a bunch of camera crews round here over the years and they do all manner of things: scampering off around the tarmac airside, going out beyond the yellow apron, you name it. But you have earnt my trust. I will allow you to work as two groups.' Aaaanyway, we have us the heck some fun, manage to stay within the yellow apron, get all the shots we need and after only about three and a half hours are strapped into a tiny aeroplane with our thousand bags around us for the four-and-a-half-hour flight to Dawson.

We've come across quite a lot of attitude from the men

we've met so far in Canada – the women, I've mentioned, possibly, tend towards big bubbly personalities (every man Jack of them), but I am genuinely looking forward to meeting one single man here who doesn't seem like he wants to start a fight. Kim, the pilot who flew us on to the lake on the first morning here, ended up being sweet as pie – positively chummy with our cameraman (they bonded over the drone camera, which is always a good icebreaker) – but not before we'd gone through any number of needless antler clashes. Our pilots up to Dawson didn't give us the time to soften, so their swords were drawn from the first moment till the last. They did very decently fly us to Dawson as we had paid them to do, but they were buggered if they were going to be nice about it. I feel entitled to make this judgement about the menfolk of one of the largest countries on our planet because I have now met three or four of them and so no one can question the rigour of my research. Is this, I wonder, related in any way to the women being so outgoing? Do the men feel undermined and therefore have to make their presence felt by walking with such a heavy tread? As I say, my work on this topic is exhaustive, so I know whereof I speak.

One might imagine that of all the varieties of Arctic landscape we'd have seen pretty much the full gamut by now – the flat white of Greenland's interior, the fearsome jab of its ice fjords, the drama of Iceland's volcanic rock forms, the flat-topped mountains of Svalbard – but our view from the aerial portholes shows another wholly new terrain of rolling hills and mountains with frozen rivers coiling rudely below like lengths of silvery intestine laid out along valley after valley, stubbled with brown conifers. I search idly for any sign of human habitation, any straight line of fence, road or plantation that might show the touch of man, but, no, for hour after hour, mile after hundred mile, this is giant, untrodden endless wilderness: a beautiful eternity of highland nothing. I conjure up sweet little villages and imagine them lolling in the nooks of such a geography. Those rivers below, sausaging their way towards some infinitely distant sea, presumably thrum with salmon – has anyone, I wondered, ever cast a fly on them in summer? There's something rather restorative about the contemplation of so much emptiness: it gives you more room mentally to swirl around the rest of life and appreciate it, like a half-inch of claret in a large-bowled wineglass.

One of the services provided by Buffalo Airways is fire control. They've got several water-spraying planes that can scooch up water (and the odd snorkeller, according to apocryphal tales from the more 'fanciful' end of the shelf) from the lakes and drop it on to the forest fires that become a constant feature of this region's summer months. Their aim, according to Pete, is 'to contain fire and protect settlements rather than extinguish fire. Right now there are a thousand fires smouldering away underground just waiting for the summer, then they'll leap right back up to the trees and whoosh we're away again, yes, sir.'

After four hours and forty-five minutes, the pilots activate the seatbelt sign, which in this tiny plane comes on with a ping like the world's angriest strongman summoning a receptionist. Every one of us leaps three inches from our seats. We are flying down into the icy wastes, and from nowhere below us, in one of the hundreds of thousands of folds in the hills, there emerges first a road, then a small low building and, beside that, an airstrip. This is Yukon Airport.

We are met at Yukon by Denis (pronounced Denn-ee, they take this French thing very seriously in Canada), who is standing on the other side of the big locked gate that leads off the tarmac. He thrusts his hand through a hip-height gap between the gates to shake all of ours, leaning in as he does so in order to get a better look at us through a shoulder-height gap. I wonder idly if Denis has lots of experience of shaking hands through bars. He has sourced a hire car for us (which apparently he had to get from Whitehorse – about five hours' drive away) and drives us into Dawson with a running commentary all the way ('See that taxi cab? That's the only cab in the city. I know 'cos I sold the business three years ago', 'All this landscape was created by the dredge', 'Moose meat is the only meat you need and it's the best an' all, 'sgot all your protein and fat and 90 per cent of your vitamin and mineral requirements too', 'Unless you absolutely have to, don't set foot in the north end o' town. Nuttin' but rough stuff goin' on there', 'There's the Chinese restaurant, 'spretty good', 'Right here's the south end o' town, it's pretty much a mixture of First Nations and other settlers. North end is all First Nations'). After several trips back and forth into Dawson – and by all accounts telling exactly the same story on each pass – he finally manages to ferry all of us, and our kit, to Bombay Peggy's, our resting place for the next three nights.

Dawson is surprisingly beautiful: a gold-rush town that sprang up on the site of a First Nations fishing camp in 1896, swelling quickly to 40,000 people at its peak in 1898 – hence its proper name, Dawson City – then waning overnight to 8,000 by 1899 when the rush was deemed to be over. 'First Nations', incidentally, is the term used to describe the non-Inuit or Métis indigenous people of Canada and the US. It's basically what we should all be saying instead of 'Indian', a word that I'm appalled to say I still have to make a conscious effort to avoid (I was educated in less thoughtful times and it has rather stuck in my stupid head). So to recap: Native American is a good general name, First Nation a specifically Canadian name, and Red Indian something to be excised from your vocabulary. For now. Dawson City has shrunk right back to about 1,200 people these days and is now just a few streets of handsome painted weatherboard houses with flat Dutch-looking wooden facades. Names and businesses are curlicued up on the fronts in fairground cowboy writing: 'Peabody's Photographic Parlor', 'The Red Feather Saloon', 'The Downtown Hotel', 'K.T.M.Co. Store That Sells Most Everything', 'Hair We Are Barbershop'.

It's a film set ready to stand in for any frontier location you may care to name: oil town, gold-rush town, mid-west cowboy town. But, extraordinarily, it is real. These houses might have been maintained in this state to please tourists or they may well not have been. They are all working businesses and a good many of them mining concerns (one advertising picks and shovels), all open and working most hours of most days. The gold rush may have ebbed and flowed a bit over the years, but this place is still full of prospectors – including (why doesn't this surprise me?) the multi-faceted Denis – who stake out claims and assess their gold content day after day.

Dawson sits, not unlike our beautiful Rothbury in Northumberland, surrounded by hills, so whichever way you look you can raise your eyes and see craggy, pine-dotted uplands. The imperious Yukon river, wider than . . . all right, not a mile but definitely a kilometre and currently frozen over – just like the Great Slave Lake – so serving more as road than waterway, sweeps past with a non-chalant wiggle in its stride. Our new temporary home, Bombay Peggy's, has also undergone a significant change in direction. It started out as one of the many old whore-houses in Dawson City, here to service (what a horrific expression) the armies of hardbitten men who came up here to seek their fortunes. Two of these houses of ill repute remain (I say remain, but they're no longer in the original line of business): Bombay Peggy's and Ruby's. Ruby's was more for the management (an 'executive' brothel, if you please), while Bombay Peggy's was a cheaper, rougher affair catering to the lowlier end of the market.

Wendy, the owner of the hotel into which Bombay Peggy's has been beautifully transformed, bought the building in the nineties when it was in the less salubrious northern end of town. The windows had all been knocked out and the whole place was in a pretty pitiful state of disrepair. She simply lifted the structure up with a crane, put it on runners and dragged it to the corner where it now stands illustriously in the very heart of Dawson's rather grand downtown. This is one of the many benefits of light, wooden-built houses with no basements and hardly any foundations – they can all just be moved around to fit into neat new streets. So as the town of Dawson changed its girth to accommodate the flighty rushers, streets of wooden houses could appear as magically and swiftly as they would then subsequently disappear (or get dragged elsewhere like a piece of heavy furniture). Fires were a frequent – and not entirely surprising – feature of a town built out of wood, and, given the Arctic conditions and moral laxity of most of the inhabitants, it's not hard to imagine how an unused building might quickly end up in someone else's log basket.

The hotel is full of photographs of frontier-period call girls, all cigarette holders and suspenders, the sepia boop-be-doop of the pictures doing its best to distract from the grimness of their lot. Bombay Peggy herself features in more than a few, a large imposing lady in her seventies (in the two slightly blurred images I saw), dressed in mannish clothes with a flared trouser and French peaked cap. The nickname apparently has nothing to do with Mumbai but rather with Shanghai, where Bombay Peggy started her career, at one time becoming the object of a besotted bomber pilot's ardour during the Second World War. He would drop presents for her from the bomb-bay of his plane (in flagrant contravention of any number of flying protocols . . .) and the name stuck. I get the impression that the prostitutes of the time were always on the lookout for a catchy moniker (Catchy Monica, for example, would . . . actually, probably not be a very good name, thinking about it). Certainly the more famous and memorable names in Dawson seem all to be from the seedier corners of its past; the casino, for example, is called Diamond Tooth Gertie's after a famed dancing girl of that name in the twenties.

I wonder if this is a Hollywood thing or just a human thing. We in Britain certainly have our own way of turning every wrong 'un from Dick Turpin to the Krays into some kind of folk hero, so maybe this is just the same thing. Even so, I'm struggling to think of any example of heritage working such a stunning sanitizing job on its shady past. I suppose Oxford has Fetid Lal's, which is a popular eatery with undergraduates when their parents come to take them out, and of course one of Harrogate's most popular attractions is Pox-Ridden Nellie's Knocking Shop, which is a small lending library.[1]

---

[1] I might have made these up.

13

Staking a Klondike Claim

Denis comes to meet us on our first morning to show us one of his claims. He pulls up later than expected (apparently 'We're on Dawson time' – oh, how I enjoy Rog's reaction to that), and we follow his pick-up to a spot about a mile or two off the highway, twenty minutes up into the hills. There we stumble on a perfectly odd little street of wooden buildings that Denis's friend and prospecting partner Alain has put up (with no small skill) to live in and house all his equipment. It's like a mini Dawson of sheds with *Bonanza* fronts. Alain has even painted stuff like 'Extra Old Stock' on to the front of one and 'Winchester' on to another in honour of his favourite beer and gun respectively.

There are other adornments too. Wheel hubs hang on one wall at the end of the street, glinting in the sunshine and every now and then clanging in the light breeze like Nepalese prayer bells. A stuffed rag doll is nailed to another wall, and for a horrid moment it crosses my mind what a sinister place this would be if Denis had brought you here against your will, bundled into the back of his car, say. I count up our number: five, including James, our 6 foot 4 inches soundman. I reckon we'll be OK if Denis and Alain turn ugly, unless they are both armed, of course, which *of course* (what was I thinking?) is exactly what they would be.

Luckily Denis and Alain are as good as the gold they're seeking (or, if they're not, at least they don't kill us). Denis talks excitedly about his ninety-seven claims further up into the Klondike wilds. He takes me stage by stage through the business of securing a claim. You just have to stake it out – literally with wooden sticks – so that you've put your name on it, then you register it and pay $10 per claim per year. You then have to start digging to the bedrock so you can send a sample of it to the assays each year to get it assessed. There are assays 'in all the big towns' (says Denis). I picture them being a cross between a public library and an enormous school chemistry lab (with a man playing a piano and lots of fiddleback chairs for smashing over people's backs) – Denis certainly doesn't offer any further explanation – but I would guess testing and filing would be the bones of it. If the assays don't hear from you within the allotted time ('One second past midnight, buddy, on the year after you bought it'), the property, and all the work you might have done on it, reverts back to the Crown – or more likely to the next prospector.

'Come see, buddy,' says Denis in a burp of beer. I'm rather warming to Denis. He looks and sounds so completely like a lovable comedy villain (with his slightly raspy, high Danny de Vito comedy-villain voice, every time he says 'buddy' I have to fight the urge to look round and see if Macaulay Culkin might be hiding somewhere, about to drop a bucket of glue and a ton of feathers on us). The claim we are on is currently being prospected by Denis and Alain through a three foot by three foot shaft they have dug about thirty foot deep into the Yukon turf, boarded up with bits of old shop signs ('teakhouse – the Best in Alas – ternationally renowned cuisi'). As Denis explains, this shafting is best done in the winter, as there are numerous underground waterways, all of which can be drilled through when they are solid but will be in full flow in warmer months.

Alain is dutifully at the bottom of the hole with a jackhammer, whose flex comes beanstalking up the shaft; every so often he stops and Denis throws down a bucket on a rope for the debris. They seem to make fairly speedy progress: the hammer can loosen about a foot of ice with each circuit of the floor. This is hauled up hand over hand ('Whoa! I've goddit, buddy!') in massive chunks of cold crystal like the sculpted plastic on the pub draught pump of a terrible lager, and another layer of ice is revealed below. This continues until they reach the bedrock, which, says Denis with fingers crossed, will be full of gold.

He fishes about in his pocket until he finds a little drawstring bag with a small medicine-type bottle in it. The bottle is carefully opened and its contents shaken out on to Denis's hand. 'Buddy, this is what we're praying for.' There on Denis's hand is a splodge of gold dust that if it could be rolled up would make a ball the size of a very small pea. How much is that worth, I wonder? 'Dunno. There's several grams here. Once purified could be 'bout six hundred to eight hundred dollars' worth.' I suddenly feel a little turn in my stomach that might be the breakfast of twelve men that I devoured just an hour or so before or could just possibly be the initial ginger stages of Gold Fever.

'Gold Fever seizes people,' Denis says with the desperate seriousness of a phone-in programme's resident doctor. 'Makes 'em do crazy things. They'll go all out for gold, maybe diggin' in the summer months, or diggin' under ice, without the proper eng'neerin', and suddenly kerpoom the whole lot comes down. Else they get stuck out in the 50-belows and no one finds 'em till the spring when they're good an' cold. I tell you another thing: you wanna make sure you trust the guy you're working with, 'cos you're down there diggin', he's up here. All he godda do is make sure you stay down there and there's one less partner to share the colour with. Buried standing up like the Chinese, he he.' Has this ever happened? (And do the Chinese get buried standing up?) Denis makes a sort of moue that says maybe it has, maybe it hasn't (and he doesn't know about the Chinese standing-up thing). So what state are your other claims in, Denis? 'Oh, they're good claims. I have gone into partnership with a Norwegian firm that's gonna mine one of my claims, startin' next year.' That's very exciting! 'Sure. Went to meet 'em and they put me up the same place as the King 'n' Queen of Norway.' Really? 'Same place.' (I do hope you're enjoying my faithful recreation of Denis's speech by the way.)

Alain and Denis have been on the beers since about 10 a.m. They've brought with them a friend of Denis's ('He's a celebrated photographer. Been to Afghanistan'), who in turn has brought his young son and a couple of puppies. The acclaimed visual chronicler of the Hindu Kush says virtually nothing all morning – well, they do say a picture paints a thousand words – preferring to stand aloof and smoke weapons-grade skunk while his poor son remains in the back of the car with the puppies for the whole morning. It strikes a faintly odd note, having this wordless family get-together on the edge of our morning. And all adds to the weirdness of the occasion.

There's no getting away from the fact that this prospecting business only really becomes respectable once there is involvement from a larger mining concern. Until that point you cannot help feeling that it is simply weaselly men with nothing better to do, scrabbling around in the dirt for treasure. These are hard men – brave men – but they're ridiculous men too, really; men who seem led too easily by something between greed and superstition. There's something appealing about Denis's talk of living off the grid up here at the claim, eating moose (with all its high RDA essentials . . .) and catching salmon from the Yukon to smoke, but at the same time there is, for me, something altogether too ropey about the whole Denis thing to ignore. His banter is an elegant slip knot of internal contradictions, like a bad alibi on a first telling. Beers have been opening all morning, and Denis (who is meant to be our ride back to Dawson) is getting drunker by the hour. The beers are Extra Old Stock, like on the sign. I am quite keen to leave before the Winchesters come out, like on the other sign.

Before we gratefully take our leave of the claim (we all pile into our small hire car rather than risk Denis's chauffeuring at this stage), Denis, sure enough, demands extra payment, putting on a bravura performance of comedy menace. Luckily the Winchesters never have to be brought from their cases: we were going to bung him a few extra dollars anyway as a tip. Only this way he gets it with slightly less good grace, but it means we're all rather relieved to be leaving. On our way home we head up Bonanza Creek Road (yes, that is its name), where they have left one of the ancient dredges that once worked the land (and created the landscape – Denis was right) here-abouts. We have to drive about eight miles up the creek, on road that is still substantially ice-bound, not really knowing what this dredge could possibly look like, only knowing – from the work it has done – that it has to be massive. We spot diggers of various sizes stuck under huge crusts of frozen snowfall at the side of the road. Might one of these be the famous dredge? No. We press on, with a hunch that the dredge will have to be more significant than that.

And then we see it. Dredge No. 4 is to the left of the

road, a huge wooden factory with – when it too is sold to be a hotel – what one would have to call Georgian-style windows. It is a monster – about the size of a football pitch and eight storeys high. It has a huge stacker belt like a proboscis, out of which the tailing piles of gravel are thrown. The landscape further down the creek between Dawson and the airport has been laid out like a horizontal stack of slanting poker chips by this monstrous croupier of the Yukon. Built in 1912, it has sloped through the region on a pond of its own creation, noshing down on the land before it and digging through the dirt at a rate of twenty-two buckets per minute, grinding with a noise hitherto only known in war and the more impressive Acts of God, through the rock, residual ice (this was 'placer' mining, a summer pursuit), gravel and silt, and throwing up clouds of mosquitoes as well as delivering, on its best ever day, over eight hundred ounces of gold.

We head back to Dawson in dazed silence. It feels like we have watched the *Fighting Temeraire* being unhulled and then stopped off at a war cemetery on our way home, travelling via the tumbledown workhouse at the end of the road. To lift our spirits, though, the sun has come out. This is only four-layer weather. Denis has said it: the thaw is coming. Certainly we've all taken our gloves off and been pleased to find none of our fingers has turned black or dropped off. Yes, we are definitely coming out of the extreme cold we have become used to. It is –7° and it feels hotter than July.

* * *

On returning to Bombay Peggy's I get a chance to talk more with Wendy, our hotel's proprietress. She runs the hotel, and her young family and a seemingly endless number of dogs (huskies, obviously) with a really rather impressive ease. She came from Vancouver originally. Strangely, I don't meet a single person in this part of Canada, including Denis (Ottawa), who was born here – they've all come from outside. Wendy, like all the others, came to the Yukon to seek her fortune and quickly decided that this rather splendid hotel would be her route to it. I think she's chosen well. It's gratifying to see that the entrepreneurial spirit of Dawson isn't exclusively confined to the gold trufflers. What I particularly love about Bombay Peggy's, though, is the huge pleasure they get from their guests' enjoyment. It's almost (if you could imagine such a thing) as if they care more about their guests than they do about the commercial side of the operation. I suspect they do spectacular business, but they go about it in such a delightful and thoughtful way that they win you over hook, line and sinker. What an excellent business model – a world away from Denis and his dodgy last-minute add-ons – this is all about going the extra mile to please your clientele. As a way of going about business it's a good deal more enriching, I should think, for the soul as well as the pocket.

While Wendy and I are talking, two women walk up to us in the street with big green apples in their hands. 'Hey, Wendy, we're all gonna go up river and make a camp this weekend. You wanna come up with your dogs and whoever? You'd be most welcome. It's just a bunch of us.' Not only is the sun out but everyone's making outdoor plans for the weekend. The women each take a crunchy mouthful of apple, and there on the Dawson boardwalk I feel the first thrum of spring.

I don't know when women came to Dawson – by which I mean the ones that weren't working the night shift. This, like all the rush towns, was a place for smelly men to get rich, drunk and laid. But at some point the bank must have been built and the store and the mining companies, all of which will have required people who actually got up in the mornings to run them. And these people will have brought their families, built the church, established the school. They will have required a governor to come and live in the attractive large house at the edge of town, the same insistent dark yellow as a hoo-ha's corduroy trousers. That, I suppose, is how these towns were saved from becoming slimy Gomorrahs.

This evening I am obliged to undergo one of the sillier Dawson City rituals: drinking the Sourtoe Cocktail. It's possibly not something I'd have put myself forward for in the normal run of things, but dammit I'm here to explore and it does add an interesting flavour to the place (in more ways than one). The Ceremony of the Toe is one performed on the most gullible and/or drunk of Dawson's visitors. They need to present themselves to the 'Sourtoe Captain' at the bar of the Downtown Hotel. The Captain is a man called Terry, dressed in a boiler suit and a jaunty cap'n's hat, with a huge silver beard and – I fear – one foot (and possibly a toe or two of the other) in the grave. He looks like the ghost of Spike Milligan but has a surprisingly youthful voice that, when it isn't racked with coughs, has a commanding edge to it.

Terry produces a wooden chest from behind the bar and totters over to the 'Toe Station'. The journey takes us past a pool game being played by a man of about twenty-two with what has to be self-cut hair hanging lankly over one shoulder but not so much over the other, and another man of about the same age with a huge passive-aggressive Mumford beard. Menace pulses from them as we pass. Haircut suddenly stops me and holds up his hand: 'High Five!' he orders. I comply, but I can't be certain my show of what-ho bonhomie will have looked remotely convincing. I am beginning to think I'd gleefully pay half of all I own to be elsewhere. We get to the Toe Station, a dark corner near the door marked by a rubbish poster showing a hand-drawn picture of an old toe. While we discuss how to shoot and light the scene, the dead man's chest is put in its rightful place and Terry sits on a chair a little way off to dodge the reaper for a few more minutes.

During this time, Pass-Ag comes over and announces that he is the manager of the bar and we will go easy on Terry or else we'll be out. Interestingly, we have no intention of going any other way on Terry and – personally speaking – I am counting the seconds till I can put continents between me and the bar of the Downtown Hotel, so he needn't worry on that score. The place is so charged with unvented aggression, and we are so obviously the only outlet, it's as though a huge thunderstorm were building and all the while with each new light stand we put up we're just raising our massive antenna even higher into the cumulonimbus. However, just in the nick of time, our secret weapon turns up in the unlikely shape of Denis, who has a sort of on/off non-specific job at the Downtown. Denis is everyone's friend; I've never seen a man bounce along so much on the spring of a full wallet – we have been the making of Denis and for that I am pleased. With Denis as our champion, we manage to get things moving and stop the mood of sullen resentment in the place sparking into outright violence, at least for now. Eventually we are ready; Terry has been restored to his proper state of Sourtoe Captain conviviality and Pass-Ag beard man has buggered off, hopefully to some quiet corner so he can take a long hard look at himself.

Terry produces all the tools for his cocktail making from the chest and lays them out carefully like a surgeon with his scalpels. Once all the flummery of the kit has been amassed, out comes a jar full of white crystals. Cap'n Terry flexes his fingers (somewhat unnecessarily – I mean, we're not cracking a safe here) before unscrewing the lid, then proceeds with immense precision to empty the coarse crystals on to a piece of paper on the tabletop, mounting them up into a neat pyramid. Just when the greatest moment of drama is upon us, a large cake of crystals from within the jar comes tumbling out, rolling off the side of the pyramid and on to the floor. 'Fuck,' says the cap'n. 'If I find out who was the last person to touch that toe, I'll fuckin' kill 'im.' I rather believe he would too.

Terry hobbles off, having picked up the hideous lump of black, toe-ish-looking flesh that had been inside the little crystal cake. I have to say at this point that I was pretty happy with the levels of weird and grizzly we had already been at before any of this caper kicked off. This new development is taking the whole experience to entirely new heights of please-can-I-go-home-now. The looks that are coming our way from Pass-Ag Mumford and Haircut right now are murderous (which seems harsh; I mean, we're only doing their stupid bloody initiation – and paying to do it too). Terry comes back with a new carton of salt crystals (so at least we've discovered what they are, fancy!) and fiddles about with the toe (because, yes, that is what the black thing was), making particular play of the stump, which has a fibrous character, like the tufty end of a snapped stick. When he's done this to his fancy, he places it on top of its salt mound and begins.

We are thrown headlong into a historical maelstrom of trappers, bootleggers and gold prospectors from the time of Prohibition onwards. A story of two brothers smuggling Over Proof rum gradually coalesces and thence the tale of how one of them got frostbite in his foot, which resulted in the other brother cutting one of his toes off and preserving it in a flask of rum. The story spins round endless relations and offspring like a story round the dining room table at home ('That was Otto M'Graw and his son – no, sorry, Carl M'Graw and his son . . .) until – thank the Lord – we get to the bit where someone or other ('Frank Hender

– no, wait, Jo Henderson') finally drinks the sodding toe. Terry (I do rather wish he was called 'Old Isaac' or 'Japheth' or something – 'Terry' doesn't really summon up the figure in front of me) lifts up the hideous relic, explaining that it had come from the hospital (legally? I wondered) a couple of years ago and has been preserved medically and then mummified – hence the salt.

My time is approaching and, frankly, it can't be over soon enough. A glass of dark rum is produced from the bar and with not a great deal of finesse the darkened digit is plopped into it. I drink the liquid down as quickly as I can, Old Isaac all the while watching to see that I break no rules (on pain of being barred from membership of the Order of the Sourtoe – like I give a toss, but strangely, weirdly, I still go along with everything he says). 'The lips have to touch the toe but you mustn't swallow it' (yeah, 'cos otherwise I'd chomp it down). Then, when I've finished, he picks up the toe and squeezes out the soggy stump end before handing the glass back to me: 'O' course I didn't tell you that to be admitted to the brotherhood, you have to drink everything, including the toe jam.' Why I don't just say no, I have absolutely no idea, but anyway I drink down the last dregs, which are salty and – I swear – a bit fleshy. Yuck yuck yuck yuck yuck yuck yuck. Eurghhhhhh. Come back grouse vodka, all is forgiven . . . well, almost all.

After the gentility of Bombay Peggy's, it's good to see this other side of Dawson and to smell a bit of genuine rough frontier spirit. This bar with its hicks and its brimming testosterone, its hairy-chinned men in hats (either ten gallon or, more likely, plastic forecourt baseball hats with mechanical- or weapons-related logos on them), any one of whom might cheerfully take on any other one if there were money in it, is what the Yukon has been all about since the gold rush started. A godless, mean barroom mob who I suspect could be stirred with a feather into something unspeakably scary if the mood was right. The last thing we have to pick up – slightly humiliatingly – is the shot of me walking into the bar that will be the opening shot of this sequence in the final edit, so I spend the next quarter of an hour being filmed from various angles walking over the road and into the Downtown Bar, turning round and walking straight out again, each time with a blast of freezing air and a slam of the swing doors. You can't imagine how much this endears me to the locals. Maybe Denis manages to calm them down, maybe they get bored of us, or maybe I am just overreacting to a perfectly normal and friendly Friday night at the Downtown, but we manage to get out of there without a single punch, glass or bottle being thrown.

Our ride to the airport the next morning is courtesy of the famous single cab of Dawson that Denis pointed out to us on our journey in. The cab is driven by Patricia, who, although we only meet her as a small part late in the story, is one of the real gems of Dawson, like a nice mint after a vicious curry.

From the tiny airstrip at Dawson we are flying across to Fairbanks in Alaska, following the Yukon River. This is our farewell to Canada. I feed the last loonies and toonies from my pockets (this is what the Canadians rather sweetly call their one- and two-dollar bits) into the drinks machine just so I can taste the Coffee Flavored Root Beer that is daring me from the other side of the glass. Fizzy Dettol is all I got from my small – and indeed only – sip. This Canadian leg of the journey has also left a strange taste in my mouth, I think, though (strangely) it's one I could come to love. The landscape here is off the scale. I took several walks out of Dawson along the Yukon Valley but never got very far because every way I turned there was another monster view that needed to be absorbed and savoured. The people are similarly large of character – I've written about them with rather a jaundiced eye, but whoever they are, whatever their business, you have to say this for them: they are all very engaging. Yes, that engagement might be a desire to punch your lights out, but better to be acknowledged than be ignored, every time.

14

Fairbanks: The Perfect
Start to the Day

Fairbanks is Alaska's second-biggest city. Flying over it before landing at the plush private charter terminal, it sprawls out like a schoolboy trying to bagsy all the back seats in a bus. We sit in the plushness of the arrivals lounge and drink 'Christmas-flavoured' coffee (that's what it said on the urn – and they were right: beautifully cinnamon-y and clove-y, although I'd have maybe pulled back on the bread sauce and Downton flavours if it were me) while two of our number go off to pick up our cars. They return twenty minutes later with one of them, the other having apparently been picked up earlier by our fixer. Yes, we now have a 'fixer' – an Alaskan called Shane, a new sixth member of the band who, strangely, is joining our tight unit for the last leg of the trip. We've been through wilds, we've been through storms, we've been through the most desolate corners of the northern globe, but now, as we enter the land of the free, we are to have a fixer. We are all concerned: concerned about the chemistry being suddenly tampered with at this late stage, concerned that he shouldn't feel excluded from our group and concerned that he might be a total bell-piece. He has now disappeared with our hire car and isn't answering his mobile. Yes, we are concerned.

After a full forty-five minutes of concern, a pick-up truck the size of a farmhouse pulls up and through its windscreen we spot Shane the Fixer: a man in his early thirties with a flat cap on his head, a pair of sunglasses on his nose and a lustrous beard a foot or more long wound into rabbinical sandy ringlets hanging from his chin like commuters from handstraps. Shane hops down with the practised agility of a wild woodland creature from the poop deck of the pick-up and explains in a beautiful, round and honest baritone – a voice that rings with the sonorous cadences of famous ancient pulpits, a voice that is fluted and scalloped with even-handed wisdom – that he's been waiting at the other terminal. We load up our thousand cases and hoof off to the hotel.

Fairbanks – enticingly known as 'America's coldest city' – is laid out in a grid. And when I say 'a grid', I mean 'a grid'. Imagine taking the London North Circular road (and South Circular, of course – in fact let's just take the Circular) and cutting it into three-mile strips. Immediately discard any of those strips that contain any greenery (I'm thinking specifically of the Ealing area, for example, where the two roads intersect in the west). Now use the strips of the Circular to make an enormous Shreddie on the ground, laying out the roads and the huge industrial metal barns and dun-coloured towers of office or residential property that loaf on either side of it. Make it a massive Shreddie, remembering of course to grid it with crossed streets. Don't worry about matching anything, because the strips you've chosen should all be remarkably similar. OK now, what you have made right there, there with your street cereal morsel, is Fairbanks. That is the whole city. It, like a Shreddie (if you've ever studied one closely), has no town centre. It has all the things it needs – shops, houses, civic buildings, offices, restaurants, hospitals, churches and schools – accommodated in those plain, low-rise barns. Acres and acres of car park fill any spaces that aren't yet barned. Roads of several lanes lead importantly from one square mile of shops the size of postal districts to the next. Fairbanks has riverbanks, many of them indeed, on the Tanana and Chena rivers, whose confluence you might have thought was the reason behind the town's location and possibly its name, but no, there's nothing fair about the banks here. The city was named after a republican senator from Indiana, Charles W. Fairbanks, who went on to become Vice President of the US under Theodore Roosevelt (good *Pointless* fact there), and was initially just a place for yet more weaselly men to gamble, drink and get laid.

The hotel we're billeted at is the Westmark. I suppose it's the best hotel in the city, in that it boasts three stars and stands impressively across an acre or two of downtown

Fairbanks just next to several dun-coloured office-type buildings and about two acres of litter-strewn car park. The Westmark looks like a colossal hospital – with spurs and add-ons and walkways and huge chimneys – which is ironic because practically every other business in this corner of the Shreddie seems to be a medical facility (despite being housed in dun-coloured office-type buildings). Bizarre.

The hotel's reception continues the hospital theme with its cafe and shop, as indeed do the endless corridors leading to different departments, all of which have hospital signage hanging from low ceilings with arrows and lists of buildings, wings and towers. My ward . . . sorry, my room is in the North Tower (the two towers are called North Tower and South Tower – why the hell not throw in a bit of 9/11 resonance just to 'up' the weird?). The hotel is full of two immediately identifiable groupings: Asian tourists (Chinese and Japanese, mainly) and Inupiats, the Alaskan relations of the Inuits of Greenland.

Like the Inuits, the Inupiat are faintly Asian in appearance, but they also have a strong Native American look, which – armchair anthropologist that I like to think myself – suddenly makes perfect sense. Of course! The First Nations people of America are related to the Inuit, who in turn are related to the ancient people of China and Mongolia. Or the other way around. Maybe everyone else has known that for ever, but it's the first time it has ever dawned on me. Eureka. Or perhaps Duh.

I have to be honest and say that the First Nation people

here at the Westmark don't look to be in good shape. For the most part they all seem incredibly infirm, many are in wheelchairs or are hobbling around – usually to get to one of the many (automatic) doors leading outside to the many car parks so they can cluster around the brimming ashtrays under the porticos for a cheeky smoke. This hospital thing is now SO strong that I begin to wonder if we aren't the butt of some tremendous practical joke. There are people with drips. Everywhere there are hand-sanitizers. But the Inupiat thing really troubles me; it's not just that they all look ill, or that they're constantly having to limp painfully outside for cigarettes, it's the fact that they all look damaged. Something horrific has happened to these people.

Could that horrific thing be Fairbanks itself? Driving around this place, the endless modules of identical city do certainly start to wear you down. It is often said of a place that it 'has no soul', but this is a place that not only lacks soul, it truly has no meaningful anatomy at all. There is no organic axis to it; no central market or square or cathedral – of course it has these elements in spades, I'm sure you can't move for markets and cathedrals of various kinds, but they're dotted about here and there in the dun-coloured office-style buildings. A friend once put me right about industrial honey production after I had been saying that honey was surely one product you could guarantee to be 100 per cent natural. Turns out it isn't. Industrial honey producers put vast quantities of hives next to vast piles of sugar, and so instead of lean bees swooning off to buzz around wafty banks of lavenders or the nodding orbs of peonies, enormous great worker bees walk uncomfortably across from their lab-hive to suck up pure sugar before waddling crossly back like stripy Elton Johns to sick up honey. Once again it's an unsettling insight into the minds of commercial food manufacturers, working on the other side from the Bombay Peggys and the Børges of this world. Anyway, this is what Fairbanks reminds me of: fat, flightless bees being drip-fed sugar and conned into thinking they are alive. I wonder if I'm just going through a particularly dyspeptic phase of the journey or if this is exactly what I would have thought if we'd come here first. I suspect the latter . . .

We keep seeing signs for North Pole, which is rather peculiar as in Fairbanks you are a good 1,700 miles away from the North Pole. Then, as we get closer, we see signs for Santa Claus Lane, Snowman Lane and St Nicholas Drive, and then, suddenly, with no warning at all, a massive fibreglass Father Christmas looms up beside the road. This we have to investigate. It turns out North Pole is a suburb of Fairbanks that is permanently Christmas themed – even the streetlights are striped red-and-white candy canes. Absolutely hilarious.

Back in the 1940s, someone came up with the idea of calling this place North Pole, hoping to lure toy manufacturers here to open factories so that they could stamp 'made in North Pole' on their products. The only flaw in the plan was that toy manufacturers, as it turns out, aren't complete idiots. They all said, 'Thank you very much but we're pretty happy where we are and tempting though it might be to move the entire operation to the edge of Weirdsville Fucking Nowhere, we're probably going to pass,' before putting the phone down and crying with laughter till they almost wee-ed. The president of the North Pole chamber of commerce has changed his name to Santa Claus by deed poll and that is everything you need to know about the sheer unfettered puerility of this place. That and the fact that busloads of Asian tourists are dropped off here and go batshit crazy for it.

Our first night in the hotel is a troubling one – hardly anyone manages to sleep. Our director and our soundman have people coming and going all night in their corridor. Outside my room, doors are slamming throughout the tiny wee hours and anguished conversations rattle on unintelligibly by the lifts. When we meet in the morning, we are raced off to a diner for breakfast, partly to remove us from the unpleasant scene in reception where someone is being led away in handcuffs by the rozzers and partly because the hotel food has been sampled by Shane the Fixer and pronounced (in mellifluous and resonant tones) 'substandard'. We ask Shane about the hospital thing and – call me Miss Marple – we're right. It turns out that the First Nations people of the area get free medical care and so are brought in from their settlements and put up for free here at the Westmark because it's so close to the treatment centres. Well, that answers that question. And, I'm tempted to think, good for the state for providing such comprehensive healthcare.

15

Dining on Beaver with David and Jenna

This morning we're heading off to stay overnight with a couple who live in the woods subsisting on what they hunt and forage. You have got to say this for Fairbanks: five minutes out of town and you're in some of the finest and most majestic scenery on earth. Maybe that's why they don't worry too much about how the city itself looks. Forty minutes up the road, we turn on to a snowbound track and find ourselves driving through spruce and birch forest. Every so often it opens up where rides have been cut through perpendicular to the road and there are huge views up wooded slopes to distant hilltops. This feels proper again and, after the synthetic mush of the last twenty-four hours, I gulp in the experience. The prospect of spending a day and a night out in the wild is beginning to feel exciting – like familiar territory even.

We drive and drive down that road, having been told that at some point we'll come across our wild-living help-meets, David and Jenna, who'll be there with their dog sled. Around each corner they fail and fail again to appear, but what a magical winding road it is, conifers holding a foot and a half of snow in their top third, footprints of foxes and, on one particular bend, three moose looking languorously on as only an animal with three foot of ruddy great antler on its head can. There is more Christmas in one needle of these pines than in all the phoney hoopla of the Yule log up the road.

As we drive, Shane the Fixer sings to us about bears. I asked him if we are in bear country. 'Oh, yes!' he trills. 'Very much so. In fact they should be thinking of coming out of hibernation any time now.' Right, so a great night to be spending out under canvas then . . . 'Oh, you'll be fine.' Glad you're so confident.

What sort of bears do we get here anyway? Polar bears? 'Oh no, grizzlies.' Right, so what do you consider a safe distance for a grizzly bear? 'Well, you should never go up to one.' Obviously. 'The rule of thumb is literally a rule of thumb – you stick your thumb out in front of you and if you can see any of the grizzly around your thumb, you're too close.'

Have you seen any grizzlies? 'Yes, I would say probably about seventy to eighty in my life. I've probably shot, I don't know, twenty?' Have you? 'Oh sure, with riot rounds. It just gives them a jump. I had a bear in my backyard that had found my strawberry patch, and he was just standing there eating them – they kinda love strawberries. I came out of my door and there he was, like 20 foot away from me. So I ran back in, bolted the door–' Bolted the door? What, in case the bear had got the hang of doorknobs? 'Well, a hungry grizzly wouldn't have any problem with a door. Anyway, so I went back out and fired a riot round right at him and he ran off. It's actually important that bears stay frightened of humans because then they're safe. It's only when they come into frequent contact with humans that they lose their fear and become dangerous. That's when they get shot for real.'

So what should you do if you're attacked by a bear? 'If it's a grizzly, you can curl up into a ball and you should be all right. If it was a black bear, then you'd have a fight to the death on your hands. But you know there's a new bear?' I'm sorry? Sing that again. 'Well, because the ice is melting, polar bears have been forced inland; you see, the ice is their natural home. And the polar bear has started breeding with the brown bear' – whoa, there's John Lewis's next Christmas ad right there – 'and the result is a "super bear" that has all the cunning and intelligence of the polar bear and all the ruthlessness of a grizzly.'

What's the difference between a grizzly and a brown bear? 'None, they're the same thing.' Ah! 'But the most scary thing about the super bear is that it doesn't hibernate, so it's around all winter.' I bet it's a lovely colour, though, sort of coffee crème. 'I believe it is.' Mmmm, a coffee bear.

After we've turned seven more bends in the road, there

David and Jenna are – good as their word – a healthy-looking couple in their early thirties, standing by the road with six dogs and a large sledge for our kit. We load up, and David and the kit disappear into the forest up a narrow trail beside the road. We follow on foot, as ever Rog lugging his camera and James his sound bag and boom mic. I suppose they must've got used to it, but on a two-mile trek like this you really don't want to be carrying much at all, and not for the first time I marvel at their uncomplaining hard work.

The trail takes us up a steep slope into a hillside of birch. Jenna, who is wearing a traditional Inupiat anorak tied tightly at the waist and going down to a rather forbidding stiff skirt below the knee, points to a burr of fungus growing darkly on the side of a birch tree. 'That's chaga,' she says. 'It's a mycelium that grows on the birch. We harvest it and you can make a drink from it. It's delicious – I live on the stuff. It's been proven to have anti-cancer properties and it's probably the best antioxidant in the natural world.'

We walk on, and as the slope lessens, the woodland changes as well.

'See here,' points Jenna. 'The birch has suddenly stopped and we're now into aspen.' It looks almost the same until you go up close and see that the paper bark of the birch has become a more solid, lime-like trunk. The algae dusting the surface is the same, though, which makes the aspen look silvery too. 'That algae's good for sunscreen; also, you can use it like baking powder.' Blimey, these guys really do this subsistence thing properly.

Every so often we'll stop when there's a bit of birch with peeling bark. 'If you ever see that, you gotta stop and peel as much as you can. Fill your pockets with it, as it's the best firelighter there is and you're always gonna run out of it just when you need it most.' I am reminded of the Arctic training with the Marines way back in Harstad, and how the chicken skin was thrown to one of the squaddies to use as further insulation, and how the guts were kept for use as bait. At subsistence level you use absolutely everything you can lay your hands on to help you survive.

By the time Jenna and I get there, David has been at their base for about an hour. The dogs have all been tied up next to their individual kennels and are sitting, politely panting and looking cute (these are lovely dogs, like the Sirius huskies we'd seen back at Constable Point – rather better disposed than Ono's miserable creatures). David and Jenna show me round the site, including the long-drop bog that has been ingeniously made by putting two raised planks side by side over a hole with a five-inch gap between them, so you sit on them, a leg on each plank approximately, and take care of business. The bog is covered by a tarp overhead but is otherwise open to the glorious view of the river sweeping past below, and indeed the glorious view of you sitting on the crapper is equally open to anyone who might be looking that way. Not a mistake they'd make twice.

Just next to a little terrace is the hut David and Jenna have dug into the hillside. Seven huge spruce beams form vertical piles around which the rest of the structure is built, smaller logs fill in the gaps and form the roof, and the earth that was dug out to clear the space has been back-filled, covering the roof too to provide excellent insulation and – after a fashion – waterproofing. There's a huge window in the wall looking down to the river and a rather snazzy door, which has been lined with an old sleeping bag around its edges to make a soft seal when closed. Everything, but everything, has been made by David and Jenna.

The door handle is a beautiful gnarl of aspen branch (made by David). We pull it open and go inside. The first thing to hit you is the smell. I think it's a pleasant enough scent, but when I remember it later, possibly smelling it on my clothes once we get back, I don't really remember it with pleasure in the way that one might woodsmoke on a jumper. The floor is covered in spruce boughs – why? 'Well, I guess it's better than walking on dirt.' I guess it is, I suppose. So under the boughs it's just earth? 'Yeah, we clean out the spruce every coupla weeks and put fresh down.' That is most of the smell, I think – the sappy, resin-y smell of the spruce (which you'd think would be delicious and fresh in a Radox bath-y kind of a way, but sort of isn't), but there is also a hefty bit of woodsmoke in the mix too. Really not an unpleasant smell, but ... I dunno. You've also got to factor in the residual smell of cooking. On the stove is a stockpot of moose bones bubbling away and a constant gurgling saucepan of chaga. I think, though I may be wrong, that I am picking up a couple of notes of unwashed hair in there too and, although very low in the mélange, it adds just enough body smell to the overall hooey to make it a bit patchouli-esque and unpleasant. Yup, I think that's it. Nothing a bottle of Timotei and a waterfall couldn't put right.

Aaanyhow, Jenna stokes up the woodburning stove (beautifully made by David from an oil drum they found floating downstream a couple of years before), chaga is duly poured out for me into a wonderful wooden mug that is approximately egg-shaped and carved out of a birch burr (by David), birch syrup (collected by Jenna and boiled down to a thick gloopy sweet liquid by David) is poured in and stirred with a wooden spoon (made by David). I sit on the double bed (David) covered in a huge black bearskin (David) and look out at the immense landscape below (God).

David sets to work sewing a coyote skin on to a piece of cloth that is then going to be incorporated into a new anorak. Clearly David and Jenna have made the rather fetching ones they are now wearing, including having shot and skinned the fox whose amber fur lines both their parka hoods. It can't be overstated – and not just to the Mods amongst you – how important the fur hood-ruff is on a parka. Winds up here are frequently strong, and when they are carrying a temperature of −30, which is perfectly possible on a normal day, that runs the total wind chill temperature up to about −50. This starts to be frostbite country and although feet seem to be the usual casualties, the nose and the skin over the cheekbones, as I found in Greenland, are also particularly susceptible. If you put your parka hood up and make a little Kenny-from-*South-Park* tunnel in front of your face, the fur keeps the wind out entirely and gives you a few inches of sanity-preserving still air in front of the face that even seems to be warmed slightly by your breath.

Jenna sets about preparing lunch for us. Huge steaks of pink salmon, caught in the Tanana below and smoked in their fish hut by the water's edge, are sliced out of their vacuum packs. The vacuum pump is one of the few pieces of machinery on their little acre of ground (it's not that David and Jenna forbid machinery, just that they try to make everything they possibly can themselves, and even with David's dexterity a carved wooden vacuum pump would be a stretch), but I think we can excuse them that – not least from an olfactory point of view – given its important role in fish preservation. Salmon and halibut roe and sour cream are spread on chunky croutons of home-made bread, and a fish chowder with potato and carrot in a moose stock is thick and sticky and delicious. Rhubarb or cranberry juice is on offer to drink, or just water.

How do they get their water? 'From the river.' Do you filter it or boil it? 'Nope, we just fill the bucket and bring it up. Hasn't killed us yet.' How long have you been here? 'Three years.' Where were you from originally? (You can bet they're not from here – seems no one is, apart from the Inupiat.) It turns out David is from Vermont, which doesn't seem an enormous leap away from here climatically, and Jenna is from near Detroit, which also gets pretty chilly. So how was that adjustment? 'Fine, I came up here, fell in love with it and never left.' Jenna has what I suppose one might call Irish colouring: bright coppery red hair, flashing blue eyes and a clear pink face that shines with enthusiasm. Her eyebrows shoot up when she is making a point, and she is very sweet – they both are; and not remotely hippyish, which is surprising (at least to me). They're too focused and pragmatic to be hippies, and lack that essential ponderousness ('free time') that hippies so cherish. You could never survive under these conditions if you weren't on it all the time, always thinking, always provisioning. Even if you came to the woods a hippy, your dependency on time-and-motion efficiency, and your schematic view of the seasons (how you never waste a journey – if you see something in January that you'll need in May, for heaven's sake pick it up and bring it with you) would quickly knock all the hippy out of you.

David says less than Jenna, at least on camera, but she is very apologetic every time she feels she's said more than her share. They are absolutely head-over-heels-to-the-point-of-almost-actually-falling-over in love with each other. Every time one of them speaks, the other gazes on with such affection that you want to cry. This woodland subsistence is so many millions of miles away from life as I live it, but there are moments when I could almost see myself slotting quite comfortably into it. Probably not in the sub-Arctic, though, and actually probably not for anything longer than . . . a month? Actually let's say a fortnight. OK, a WEEK, there we go, I could do it for a week very happily then I think I'd go a bit bonkers. The rhubarb juice

234

would probably be the clincher. But I still get some kind of healthy glow simply from seeing that David and Jenna are doing it and can do it perfectly healthily, so if all else fails I do at least know that I could run off and live in the woods in a kind of *Brendon Chase* way. As long as the woods had a good cellar. Like the ones in Oxfordshire do.

After lunch, Jenna and I have some butchering to do. Spring has announced its approach, and so nature's deep freeze is effectively about to be unplugged. This means there is a lot of larder housekeeping to be done. Jenna hangs up two caribou legs; she works on one and I on the other. We have to skin them with knives (made by David) like the mezzaluna ulu knives we saw in Greenland, taking the leg fur off by slicing along the point at the back of each leg where the grain of the fur meets in a kind of Mohican, and then using the knife carefully to pare away the sub-cutaneous fat as we peel the fur off. This pelt is going to be smoked to preserve it and then made into gaiters (or 'mukluks', as Jenna likes to call them). Next we have to cut away all the meat from the leg – this can be used to make mince, burgers or even dried into a chorizo sausage. Once the leg is stripped of all meat, we cut away the sinews – these get dried out to be used for sewing and are perfect if you're working with heavy materials like hides or the thicker furs. When the leg is truly bare, the hooves are removed and set aside for a native friend of Jenna's who makes them into jewellery. Finally the marrow is removed (because it's delicious), then the bones are sawn up, boiled for stock and fed to the dogs, who eat every last scrap of them. You would have to use forensics to find anything of the caribou that hasn't been put to use.

While the actual butchery is not for the squeamish, and I daresay some people might find it distasteful, I return (like the terrible pub bore that I am) to my text for the seal episode in Greenland. This is a respectful end for this caribou – not a scrap of it has been wasted. If you eat meat, there is no more honest, humane, sustainable and eco-logically sound way of doing so than by killing it yourself – legally – in the wild. Interestingly, Jenna has been a vegetarian for most of her life and still considers herself to be of a vegetarian mindset. She cares very much about animal welfare but accepts that she depends on animals for warmth, shelter and food, so when she eats meat she makes sure it is meat that she has killed cleanly herself and that the animal's life has not been taken cheaply. I entirely understand and respect that viewpoint.

My butchering duties done, I join David to help him with his sewing. He has nearly finished putting the fur ruff on the new anorak. He stitches with careful artistry; his stitches are tiny and close together, as regular and straight as if they've been sewn by elves (operating very sophisti-cated heavy machinery). David hands me two caribou skins, one of which has come from the same caribou I've just been prepping for a shepherd's pie. They need stitching together. In fact they are going to be the pad I'm sleeping on tonight, so they really do need stitching together. David and I make a companionable sewing bee for a couple of hours, chitchatting and occasionally admiring our handi-work (in David's case) or our progress (mine).

At the risk of sounding a bit Enid Blyton, there really is nothing like the gentle pleasure of making steady progress in a useful task. The sun sinks gently in the clear blue out-side, the light on the frozen Tanana gets prettier and prettier, we slurp on our chaga and look out and feel bloody marvellous. It is one of those moments of distilled happiness that occasionally settle around you. I think I generally feel happiness retrospectively – I look back and colour my memories accordingly. The past is poetry, the present as I live through it is generally stolid prose. But this is poetry in the present. I wonder if that's a common feeling when you slow down the rhythm of your life from its usual frantic drum 'n' bass to a pastoral andante? Or maybe it's just a side effect of the chaga . . .

With the sun going down, it is time to make camp. David produces a tent (made by David), and we load it and a log stove (made by David) on to a sled with a beautiful prow (made by David) curling up like an old Persian slipper. We career down a fairly treacherous slope to the frozen mudbanks of the frozen river. David issues me with an axe (bought – don't know how that fell through the net) and a pair of snowshoes (made by David). This feels like proper pioneering kit – the first time I have ever worn the strange lacrosse/tennis racquet shoes of *Boy's Own* yarns. We make our way – David very elegantly, me like an eager clown – into the forest to select some spruces to be our ridge pole and supports. I am instructed in the way of felling (the chief rule is to kneel so you don't chop your leg off below the knee – good tip) then throw about twenty blows from the axe at the stick-thin trunk until the spruce obligingly bows solemnly towards the ground. David does the next one, bringing it down in three blows aimed with millimetre accuracy. David's axe skills are weirdly dexterous – I've never thought of the axe as a precision tool, but in David's hands it can be a delicate snipper of branches, weaving up the bough like a trout upstream, or a plane taking the nicks off a whole tree's bark in thirty seconds, or simply a ruthless felling tool – everything done with perfect accuracy and in a blur of efficient strokes. At these sorts of temperatures you just can't afford to fanny about.

I fanny about trying to pick up the spruce boughs as they fall all around us. David just says, 'No', chops down a willow and with two deft Bruce Lees of his axe he's made a long willow hook on to which all the spruce boughs can be laid in a pile so they can be picked up and carried over the shoulder in a neat, heavy bundle. We fix the poles into a tripod, slide our ridge pole through the tent canopy and pin it all up, tying it fast on to the sprigs of ground willow all around us. The last thing to go in is the stove, with its clever chimney pipe that feeds up through a metal plate we slide into the door flap. The tent mostly doesn't have a floor, or at least it has a small foot or so of material that comes in at the bottom of each tent wall, so we have to cover the snow floor with a generous seven or eight inches of spruce boughs. This will give us a bit of insulation from the permafrost and a bit of spring, ideally. Then, on top of the spruce, we lay our pads of caribou skin. Caribou (cousins of the reindeer, old schoolfriends of the red deer) have wonderful hollow fibres in their fur, which makes it a particularly good insulator, but the furs are also thick, so there's quite a bit of give in them too. This is lining up to be a much more comfortable night out under the stars than the last one in Greenland.

Once camp is pronounced ready, a figure appears on the frozen river with a sled pulled by a couple of dogs. Is that Jenna? I squint. 'I guess,' says David. 'Unless there's some other super-cute girl who's just decided to appear in the forest.' Awwwwww.

We light a fire and get going with our supper – to which end Jenna produces a mammoth leg of beaver and a bowl of dough. The beaver is hung from a stick at the edge of the blaze, we all take a small ball of the dough, roll it into a worm, then coil it around the end of a straight willow stick and stick it over the heat like a marshmallow. It takes longer than one might imagine, but soon these white bull-rushes start to smell enticingly of hot baking bread.

Let's talk about beaver, though. I have never even thought of the beaver as being something for the table. Jenna and David, for whom it is one of their absolute favourite things, have been living in the woods for so long that they evidently don't find anything remotely snigger-worthy about the endless flow of beaver chat. But I'm ashamed to say 'How's your beaver, Jen?', 'So, Xander, have you ever eaten beaver before?', 'Wow, that is one massive beaver', 'Hon, why don't you share that beaver round?' etc.,

etc., etc. have me summoning every last drop of my resolve to avoid exploding with childish laughter. And as for the taste – well, it's a very strange one. It's definitely a red meat, so I'd put it into a beef/lamb/venison kind of a bracket. Someone says duck, but I don't really get that, nor pork, which is the usual catch-all for unknown meat styles. It isn't entirely unpleasant; the meat is steak-like in texture and its taste runs in that sort of direction and without being gamey, thank goodness, but the fat that runs from it has a sort of (woody? Stands to reason) flavour that you could probably learn to love, but I didn't so much. Given the size of the joint, it must have been a pretty mature beaver, and maybe a younger animal would taste better, in the way that if mutton were cooked this way it wouldn't taste as good as lamb. So perhaps I don't taste it at its best; even so, I won't be rushing back to beaver. So to speak.

The stove in our tent does a fabulous job of warming it, and when Rog the cameraman and I turn in it is toasty. Tonight the Northern Lights are the best we've seen yet. Rog set up a camera on time lapse and at first nothing seemed to be happening, but I stumble out for a tactical last-thing pee (I'd been knocking back chaga since lunchtime . . .) and see what seems to be an early glow. This quickly builds into an unbelievable sky-full of twisting cords of green light and – for the first time – a bit of red. We stay out and gawp for over an hour before finally worming our way into our sleeping bags. The last thing we do is fill the stove with logs and close the door so it can gently smoulder through the night. Three minutes later our tent is as cold as any stone.

I spend the night turning and turning. The cold of the snowy floor is by no means held back by the spruce sprigs nor even the caribou hide, so while you can be warm in your core, whichever bit of you is actually bearing your weight sucks up all the cold from the floor it is pressing against. I try to work out if it's better to sleep on my side, so it's just my hip that is going gently cryogenic, or lie on my back and spread it about a bit more evenly. I reckon the side is a better bet. From about 3 a.m. the chaga starts making its presence felt again, but my only way out of the tent would be literally to walk on Rog's pillow and if he is asleep it would be deeply unfair to wake him up, so I lie and think of deserts and dry river beds until shortly before five when – joy of joys – I hear Rog getting up to relight the fire. We've had enough of the sodding cold so just pile up the logs and watch it burn through the open door. Once again that weird maternal warm thing happens – the sense that heat is almost like a loving parent, so great is the kind of Stockholm syndrome the temperature has over you.

The morning comes beautifully and we breakfast on a sort of omelette thing and chaga with espresso shots in it, which are extremely welcome. The thrill of survival (and, if I'm honest, returning to civilization with its baths, and soap, and bed, and laundry, and warmth, and Internet, and loos, and booze, and knives and forks, and normal food, oh and mugs that aren't made of wood) is bubbling up inside us from the minute we leave the tent.

16

Forever Chris Young: With the Ice Road Truckers on the Dalton Highway

Ahhh the Westmark, drinks are free. Fun? Sunshine? Well, probably enough for everyone! Or is there? My first night back at Fairbanks' premier hotel/hospital combo is a troubled one. I'm woken at about midnight by the anguished screams of a boy in the next-door room. Something about the commotion tells me it can't just be night terrors – the screams are at that kind of convulsive, peak fury that my children reserve for only their very finest tantrums. The boy is shouting words that I can't quite make out but with a kind of sinuous ferocity that is extremely unsettling. As I listen, though, I can hear adult voices in there too, and their tone is light and conversational, so my half-asleep mind decides there is no cause for alarm. This is a medical facility of sorts, so I daresay there's a perfectly satisfactory explanation for what's going on. And, besides, there were the adults in there – someone seems to be keeping an eye on things. In any event I'm certainly not going to go next door to investigate, nor am I going to complain to the hotel front desk. I am simply going to try to ignore it and go back to sleep and then moan about it to the crew when we get up. I am English, after all. I do go back to sleep but am aware of the noise going on for three or four hours.

The next morning, Shane takes us to a diner for break-fast. We've become rather fond of one just around the corner called, rather coquettishly, 'The Diner'. Friendly waitresses bring coffee around to fill the thick china mugs of all the breakfasters with the rigour of exam invigilators supplying paper. We sit in our booth feeling all *Happy Days* and order pancakes and bacon with maple syrup. I am still clinging to the conscience-salving fallacy that I'm burning through thousands and thousands of calories in the extreme cold and therefore need to stock up on all the carbs I can lay my greedy chops on. If I carry on following this 'Mattin diet' without 'upping the gnarl' on the activity front, my wife may mistake me for a modest National Trust house on my eventual return to England.

One of the things I've noticed since being in Alaska is that if you say 'Thank you' to someone for, let's say, bringing you a foot-high pile of pancakes, instead of replying 'You're welcome' or 'It's a pleasure', they say 'You bet!' or 'Sure!' or

'Right on!' or simply a super-friendly 'U-huh!' as if, instead of saying 'Thank you', you've actually said 'Is this for me?' It's quite fun, especially from the lugubrious barman at the hotel-spital who looks at you with his hangdog bottom lip and says 'You betcha!' in a kind of country way. But it makes absolutely no sense at all; you might as well say 'Thank you' and get the response 'Paul Shane!' or 'Thank you' ... 'Chihuahua!' I suppose it's just one of those peculiar things that take root in the wrong place and grow, like a sapling in a gutter.

In the gap between ordering our immense breakfast and its arrival I tell my tale of the night before. Shane listens carefully, nodding like one of ZZ Top listening to a playback in the studio, before pronouncing in his sing-song baritone, 'That, Xander, was probably an exorcism. It is,' he sings, 'very common for native Alaskans to bring their children into town to see a witch doctor or priest.' You're saying that was an exorcism taking place in the room next to mine last night?! 'In all likelihood, yes,' he intones. Whoa. That's fairly horrific whichever way you look at it. The noise coming from Room 833 last night was a brute howl. I shudder to think of what was going on just feet away from me. That would mean those calm voices I'd heard and had thought so reassuring must have belonged to the adults who were overseeing these horrors. I suddenly feel rather stupid and a little bit sick. Exorcism is simply not the kind of thing you expect to stumble across in a hotel in America. I'd been wondering how the hotel could possibly have been less appealing. Now I have my answer.

Happily we aren't going to be staying there tonight, although there is one small catch. What we're going to be doing instead is taking our lives in our hands on a trip up the Dalton Highway. The Dalton is the infamous ice road that runs up from Fairbanks to Deadhorse and the oil-fields of Prudhoe Bay on the Arctic Ocean. It was built to service the Trans-Alaska pipeline that runs next to it every foot of its 414 miles, and it's generally thought to be one of the world's most dangerous roads. The dangers come in various fun forms: there's no mobile phone signal (all right, not exactly deadly – there are plenty of parts of central London that can make the same boast – but out in the wilds it all adds to the jeopardy); there's nowhere to stop and refuel along the whole length of the road apart from one truck stop at Coldfoot (don't you just love the snazzy names!); it's covered in ice, obviously, which just adds another layer of hairiness; but its chief danger is its traffic. This is the path of the famous Ice Road Truckers who barrel up and down to Prudhoe at terrifying speed and momentum, dragging humungous industrial loads. None but the bravest truckers do the Dalton Highway, and they are paid huge sums for the risks they take lugging supplies for the oil industry: pipes, diggers, diesel, generators, in fact just about anything you would imagine to be too big to fit on to a truck's low-loader seems to be their bread and butter.

The trucks themselves are beautiful. Their socking great cabs with long and elegant snouts give them a rather lovable, old-fashioned look – unlike our flat-fronted lorries in the UK. We see rank upon rank of them serrying (that's what ranks do, after all) at the Hilltop truckstop – our rendezvous with Otis, a Dalton pilot – all chugging away, even when parked up, presumably so they don't get cold (or else they might never start again and with NO PHONE RECEPTION that would be to invite death). They're all painted with their owner's or driver's names surrounded by jets of flame and cheery slogans like 'Burnt out and broke but still haulin' ass'.

The Hilltop is everyone's last chance to fuel up before Coldfoot, and its cafe is famous for its pies ('They do a chicken puff and a number of different berry pies,' carols Shane thoughtfully), so you would be mad on at least two counts not to stop there. Beyond that, though, it also serves as the social hub for all these great shippers of the highway. Inside the truckstop itself, in the smokers' dining room (how many places are there still in the world where your right to eat while smoking is so exquisitely preserved?) Otis shows me the memorial wall, covered with plaques commemorating Dalton truckers who've died.

Did they all die out on the Dalton? 'Not all o' them, but some.' He leans in to study the names. 'He did, and him, yup and those three did. In fact I think all of these guys did, but not her, for example, she died down in Anchorage.' There are female truckers on the Dalton Highway? 'Sure, plenny. I know two more that need to go up here from a couple months back. There was a collision, one guy died in hospital, the other was OK, but while he was in they discovered he got cancer and he died within the month. They were best buddies too. How d'you like that?'

In the corner of the smokers' room is the noticeboard. 'This is where you learn what's goin' on along the highway. If it happens on the Dalton, it goes up here.' Otis points to about thirty little paper chits pinned up on the board. 'See these? These are thank-you slips . . .' I look closer and each one has a message written on it, like '$20 for Kal Baker, thanks a million buddy for helping me with the green light Tuesday' or '$50 for Max. Really appreciated your help last week'. This is how the truckers repay their friends for kindnesses out on the road: they put money behind the bar at the Hilltop, presumably to go towards one of the many pies. There's one up there for Otis too − $40 for helping someone. 'It's kinda nice. Nowhere else does it, just Hilltop.' I don't really know what I'd expected the world of Dalton trucking to be like, but the picture that is beginning to emerge is of a much warmer and more cooperative community than I might've pictured. The truckers themselves do have a kind of swagger about them − the machismo of haulin' ass must be part of its appeal − but they're a bigger-hearted bunch than you might initially expect. Everyone we meet on the Dalton goes out of their way to be courteous, and the mutual respect amongst the truckers is very touching.

I climb up into the cab of Otis's pilot truck. It's a monster pick-up with orange flashing lights on its roof and copious little reminders of how important Otis's job is: fluorescent jackets, survival blankets, flares, traffic cones. The set-off from Hilltop takes us out on to a road called Eliot, which, although part of the Dalton Highway, isn't the Dalton proper – that doesn't start for twenty miles or so. You know when you're on to the Dalton because the road surface beneath the ice changes to gravel with only very occasional patches of paved road. If I say I've been looking forward to driving on the Dalton, what I mean is that I've been fascinated to know what the Dalton is like. What I'm really looking forward to is having driven on the Dalton (if you see what I mean). The most dangerous part of any trip abroad is never the flight you might take in any plane or helicopter, nor is it when you decide, a thousand miles inland, to 'try the seafood paella', it's when you climb into a car or minibus; it's always the roads that are the killers. This road had already demonstrated its awesome power to take lives – it is not something to be driven lightly. Or maybe it is – maybe driving lightly is the answer.

Otis drives very lightly. After about ten seconds in his pilot truck, I know I don't really have anything to worry about and I can just sit back and enjoy this colossal journey up through Alaska's wildest country. Otis can take care of the road – it's what he does, after all. The CB radio is something I dimly remember being popular in the UK in the eighties, mainly on the back of the film *Convoy*, or something like it. Maybe it's still used by truckers buzzing up and down the A1 so they can say hi to each other or make assignations at Little Chefs, I don't know. But the CB on the Dalton is a vital part of your armoury. Otis has not one but two radios fitted: one is a VHF, so we can talk to the production car behind, driven by Shane, the other a CB picking up all traffic for about a mile in any direction. The handsets live up on a clip fixed to Otis's rear-view mirror and are on neat little drawstrings that boing them back up when he lets go. To start with Shane is right behind us, and his frequent CB broadcasts are full and fruity (I think he's quite enjoying having other Alaskans to say things like 'Right On!' to) but, after a bit, I start to hear nervousness creeping into his voice and I notice he drops back until the production car is no longer behind us in any meaningful sense.

The first other Ice Road-users we come across are breakdown vehicles. These are souped-up low-loaders with flashing lights travelling north like us. My heart sinks, as we settle in behind them in Otis's nippy truck, at the thought of having to overtake in these conditions. Or maybe you don't! Maybe you just have to sit it out behind whichever Dalton beast looms up in your windscreen. 'There's been an accident up at Mile 59, so that's where they'll be headed,' Otis explains. How do you know that? 'Was on the CB about an hour ago.' Wow. 'Yeah, you gotta remember there's trucks passing through every part of the highway every couple minutes. We're all on CB, so we all get to hear about stuff pretty much as it happens.' Right you are then. Rather proving his point, he pulls down a handset. 'Ben, you OK there?' A voice comes through: 'Yup, Otis, we're good. Jus' headin' up to 59. You wanna pass you're good 'n' clear.' 'OK, I might just walk slowly round . . .' Otis duly pulls out and we overtake our first vehicle on the Ice Road. Overtaking with the help of your overtakee just takes all the danger out of it. Well, some of it anyway.

Just to keep us on our toes, we come across our first accident after only ten minutes or so: a car full of Japanese tourists has spun across the road and through a crash barrier and is now hanging precariously over a long, steep drop. Happily no one seems to be badly hurt, but they're all out of the car (good move) and standing on the road (surely less good). We slow down and Otis cranes round to see what's what. We don't stop but Otis is straight on the CB. ''kay Ben, got another job for you. Just on the corner before 16 there's a car that's over the barrier on the right-hand side.' 'OK, thanks, Otis, you keep well now.'

Does this happen regularly? 'Yeah, it's pretty common. Especially at this time of year.' How come? 'Well, the ice is starting to melt and there are patches of it that are pretty slippy, and if you don't know what to look for you can just spin out like that.' So what are the best conditions for this road? 'Winter,' replies the wily pilot without a second's hesitation. 'Then the road is covered with smooth ice, and when it's winter the ice is dry – it's a perfect driving surface, like driving on a painted road. Makes a beautiful sound. The truckers all like it too because their trucks stay clean.'

Every truck we pass has a wave for Otis and more often than not a voice comes on to the CB seconds later: 'So, how's Otis this fine morning?' Two things become clear: the first being that Dalton truckers love their CBs – or maybe they simply love talking to each other – either way no one does it without giving it a bit of brio; the second is that Otis is an important and much-loved figure on this road. Sitting in his cab and hearing all the cheery back and forth ('Oh, I'm just taking a film crew from Europe up to Coldfoot.' 'You gonna be famous, Otis? You gonna be in the movies?'), you realize that what makes this forbidding stretch of road and all its many dangers bearable is the warmth of the human contact in this elite little convivium of drivers.

We pull around a corner and see before us a huge half-mile of bridge over the Yukon (strange to think that this is the same river that swept past Dawson all those hundreds of miles away). This is going to be our first stop so that our drone camera can go up and film the picturesque gorge and its wood-plank bridge as we roll across. There's a car park with drifted-up cabins on the far side, so we come off the road there. Every truck parked in the place comes on to the CB to talk to Otis the minute we turn in. One driver, Max, who is Otis's next-door neighbour in Fairbanks, walks over for a proper face-to-face chat. Max looks about ten but is in fact twenty-six ('He's the youngest trucker on the Dalton by a country mile'). I'm going to have to revisit all my preconceptions about truckers; I've got them all wrong. 'I'm just beginning to recognize your new truck, Max, with those yellow things on the side.' 'Yeah, those are headlights, Otis, one day everyone'll have 'em.' Otis chuckles, but Max also has more serious things to discuss. Max is evidently the guardian angel of the famous accident at Mile 59. The trucker involved was a guy named AP, who seems to be a good friend of everyone's, including Otis.

The good news is that AP is fine, but we gather from Max that the 'fifth wheel' (come on, don't say you don't know what that is) must have sheered off his truck as the trailer behind him (in this case a tanker containing tens of thousands of gallons of diesel) had come free from the fixing plate on AP's cab and careered off the road, flattening about a hundred metres of woodland before coming to a rest on its side, partly buried in the tundra. Max was the first on the scene, so immediately syphoned off the diesel from the stricken tank into the empty tank he happened to have on his truck (he was on his way back from a delivery – lucky . . .) to avoid any ecological disaster (quite pleasing to see how high this comes in their priorities), and is waiting to see what is required of him now he has taken on someone else's pricy load. Again, it's extraordinary the seemingly bottomless kindness extended to a friend in need. If we were at sea, Lloyds Open Form would come into play and the stricken cargo would now belong to Max, as he'd rescued it. I'm interested to see what happens in the noble world of trucking. It seems you do what you damn well have to to help your friends, and if that means spending the rest of your day hanging around trying to make sense of a film crew 'from Europe', then so be it. I guess there'll be a slice of berry pie with Max's name on it back at Hilltop.

By the time we get to the accident, some three or four hours after it happened, we've heard pretty much everything there is to know about it courtesy of the CB. As we pull up, Ben the tow-truck guy is all in place with a winch and is hauling the empty tanker up from its resting place on to the road. AP is standing around and it all seems to be happily resolved: no one has been hurt, by some miracle – if the sheered load had spun off the other way into oncoming traffic and not aimlessly into the woods, who knows what might have happened? 'Well, AP wouldn't have let that happen if he coulda possibly helped it, y'see,' explains Otis. 'That's one of the jobs of the Ice Road Truckers: you do what you have to to keep your cargo safe, even if that means putting yourself between it and trouble.' These truckers are pretty extraordinary people.

During the second half of the journey, Otis and I discover a common enthusiasm for country music, and he unearths the CD collection that is his constant companion on trips up and down the world's most dangerous road. It is full of favourites: George Strait, Alan Jackson, Garth Brooks, Faith Hill, Keith Urban, Dierks Bentley. We put on some Chris Young and sing along as we speed past the landmarks of the Dalton – Beaver Slide, the Roller Coaster, the pertinently named Oh Shit Corner – and look out at some of the finest scenery the world can show you through a windable window.

If Otis ever feels that the piloting (and the more than decent money he makes in that line – $500 a day basic) isn't paying the bills, he wouldn't be a terrible country singer. Country music always has to be sung by an authoritative voice (in the same way that flamenco singing always has to have a hoarse voice). You can't listen to country music without picturing its vocalist sitting comfortably on a tall stool, smiling winningly out at a bar full of cuddling couples and hair-trigger fighters alike. Your male country singer needs to have the resonant worldly wisdom of a seasoned storyteller and a calm, deep voice full of warm and dependable personality. It's the same with airline pilots: they couldn't do the job unless they had the right voice, sonorous, measured and considered, otherwise the whole plane manifest would rise up as one and march on the cockpit with burning rolled-up in-flight magazines to seek redress. Otis is the very embodiment of that country spirit; he'd fit right in on any tall stool in the lower forty-eight states, roadhouse couples could sway and fall in love and rednecks could merrily glass one another as he sang.

Alaska is a very strange frontier outpost of the US, but this road-to-nowhere journey feels like the very essence of the American experience. And all the while the Trans-Alaska pipeline matches us yard for yard, unerringly somewhere within a few feet of the road, riding for the most part on raised columns at 100-foot intervals with four heat-breakers (at least I think that's what they're called – you get them on the back of a fridge) on each one to ensure that the ice at permafrost level below doesn't raise or lower the columns too much, and pumping barrel after thousand barrel of black gold. It is an oddly comforting feeling in such a fearsome wilderness to have literally millions of dollars of both construction and delivery as your soundless companion every step of the way. The pipeline is patrolled and screened by official security as well as by the unofficial eyes and ears of the truckers, but it still feels like a very exposed artery of the Western world, an uncharacteristic contract of trust with the public on the part of the US government. As far as I know, no one so far has tried to attack it, apart from the idiot who fired a rifle round at it and caused a leakage a few years ago. He – extraordinarily enough – was caught and sentenced to a calamitously long (and, they hope, salutary) stretch in prison.

Shortly before Coldfoot we pass the scene of another massive truck crash. This took place the week before and has already become notorious in Dalton CB lore for being the site of a massive diesel spillage. Clearly there was no Max on hand to take care of syphoning off the load and so three thousand gallons has glottalled into the soil. Reassuringly, though, and at a CB-estimated cost of $5 million, the land around the crash site is now being thoroughly decontaminated. Indeed, many of the trucks we've passed on our journey north have been carrying diesel-tainted earth down to Fairbanks to be incinerated.

Who pays for that? I ask. 'Oh, the truckers' insurers, for sure.' Not that many years ago, I suspect such spillages would have been swept under the carpet, so it's a great leap forward that we now live in a world where the big boys can't just run away from such things and where everyone actually cares. 'This is not National Park yet – we come into National Park around Coldfoot – but this is land that we look after very seriously,' says Otis.

Coldfoot, like most places up here, was founded at the

turn of the twentieth century and, despite the soul-freezing climate of the place, the cold feet in question actually refer to a loss of resolve rather than the more readily imagined frostbite. The landscape around Coldfoot is, for my money, the most spectacular in a state of already vocabulary-stretching natural beauty. The glens and crags and the commanding beauty of the Cheviots are all I can think of. At one point we even pass a mountain with the gentle saw-tooth skyline of Simonside, the hill above Rothbury and the most beautiful view I know, and it fills me with a vibrant and almost burning joy. As we pull off the road, Luke Bryan is on the radio singing a country hymn to 'rain' (it apparently makes the corn grow, therefore makes whisky, which in turn gets his girl 'frisky') 'Rain is a good thing . . .' he affirms. Well, quite.

Coldfoot is a magnificent truckstop – a large canteen complex with a hotel of about eighty bedrooms run by (as far as I can work out) a sorority of friendly women in a uniform that looks remarkably and unenviably like prison clothing. The canteen is a bustling and good-humoured place that is strangely full of Chinese tourists, padding out the notable presence of the roadsters like a subtle metal setting around big crusty jewels. There are men with fairy-tale beards and ten-gallon hats, men with wiry frames and baseball caps, men in tartan shirts, men covered in tattoos, men the size of trucks, men the build of bicycles. It's like the opening day of a poker tournament and everyone is bringing something strong to the party.

The hotel itself is a complex of Portakabins, each room

having a kind of backstage-at-Glastonbury feel to it, but it is bliss. It has everything you need and nothing more: a warm and comfortable bed, a basin, a loo and a shower, there are even hooks on the wall so you can hang everything up. It is one of my favourite places on the entire trip. Luxury is all rather marvellous, but there are times when 'enough' beats 'a feast' into a cocked hat.

As we're turning in that night, we run into another British film unit – it's sort of hilarious to see a group of people with a set of protocols and equipment that so closely mirrors ours. There's the sound guy with his bag and boom mic, the cameraman with his gimbal and the AP, also in a blue coat (just like ours!), with her bag full of release forms and travel admin. We nod and compare notes, cameras and agendas briefly before saying a cheerful goodnight. They are a natural-history unit up here to film the tagging of the caribou. It is one of the strange things about film crews: you can go to the most remote places in the world and just as you're about to start turning on the perfect shot, another gang from London or Bristol will emerge with their blue coats and boom mics, right on the edge of frame.

17

There's Remoteness, and Then There's Anaktuvuk

The next day we are due to meet up with Greg, a bush pilot who is going to fly us out from the tiny landing strip at Coldfoot to Anaktuvuk Pass, where there is a remote Alaskan Native settlement. The question of what the correct name is for the native peoples, incidentally, is an interesting one because it changes constantly. In some contexts, for example, the word 'native' would be thought deeply offensive, but here it seems to be a badge of pride. When I ask one of our contributors how he would describe his ethnicity, he says 'Alaskan Native' without hesitation, so that seems a pretty good endorsement of the phrase. If you use the word 'Eskimo' in Greenland, you will cause great offence; there the correct word is 'Inuit'. But in Alaska, 'Eskimo' is perfectly acceptable, even desirable, and

'Inupiat' (the Alaskan equivalent of 'Inuit') is hardly used at all. It's an area where one treads very delicately.

The bush pilots are a lifeline for these outlying communities – many of them, including Anaktuvuk, have no roads at all and so are only accessible by plane or helicopter. The bush pilots are therefore postmen, milkmen, grocery deliverymen, builders' merchants suppliers, car importers, heavy plant suppliers, buses, undertakers, pharmacists and paperboys all rolled into one. Greg is not quite what I was expecting – a tall thin man in his early thirties with glasses and a pronounced Adam's apple. He has the cold stare of an unpopular new geography teacher and when he talks us through the pre-flight safety procedures delivers much of it in a menacing whisper. He forbids any filming in the cabin, insisting that all equipment has to be stowed. He's the first and indeed only pilot on the entire series to do that: 'FAA rules,' he insists.

This is a shame, as the flight out to Anaktuvuk is yet another new high-water mark in icy beauty. It's the sort of landscape that lets you know how impossibly bloody cold it is with just a glance. All edges are crisp and strict, mountains jut obligingly with topographical lantern jaws below and in fact beside us, and frozen lakes the colour of Brad Pitt's cataracts reflect the dull light of a cloudy sun back up to us. There are no little shrubs at this point, nothing at all breaking through the regimented straight lines of hard-edged white. This is a landscape that might have been made by Greg himself.

We fly for about forty minutes, then suddenly bank steeply and drop down to a small nook at the head of a crusty lake topped with marbled ice. Only at the last minute do we see the tiny cluster of buildings and landing strip of Anaktuvuk. We've dispatched Shane the Fixer and Hermione, our AP, to drive back down the Dalton to Fairbanks, where we'll meet them later, but before they left Shane intoned a pious warning kontakion about the settlement. 'There is a funeral today, which is a very solemn occasion in Anaktuvuk – really not a good day at all for you to be going. I've spoken to the principal of the school there, and he is happy for you to go there and talk to him, but they don't want any of the children to be on camera. It's worth pointing out that like all Native settlements, Anaktuvuk is dry; under absolutely no circumstances should you take any alcohol in, even if it's just in your bag and you're taking it on for your own use. OK? Oh and I've ordered a bunch of pizzas and fish hooks for you to deliver.' Excellent, ok.

The chaos that awaits us on . . . Sorry, wait a minute. Shane, did you just say 'pizzas and fish hooks' there? 'Oh, yes, I did, they really love pizza so I've ordered two dozen 21-inch pizzas, and they need fish hooks for ice fishing, so I've got those too. You can deliver them and they'll be stoked.' Right on.

The chaos that awaits us on landing is partly due to the fact that we don't really know what we're supposed to be doing and there is no one there to meet us, and partly due to the fact that Greg is frantically unpacking all our stuff so he can get away as quickly as possible (I'm guessing he has homework to mark or some kind of rally to attend). A man with terrible teeth and a jutting underbite, who goes by the unlikely name of Jeremy, takes all our stuff and puts it in the back of his enormous pick-up before telling us quite crossly that he has no idea who we are or what we are doing here.

And then out of nowhere (pretty much like everything must be in Anaktuvuk) another man called Pat turns up and announces he's 'from the school'. Pat seems to know something about who we are, which is a relief, but he's still none the wiser on the whole 'what we are doing' front. He agrees to take us to the school, so we unload all the pizzas and fish hooks and our thousand cases of camera stuff from Jeremy's pick-up and put it into Pat's truck, the back of which seems to be mostly filled – glacier style – with densely packed frozen snow. Pat also berates us for coming on such an inopportune day, as the school bus has broken down and so he is going to have to use his truck to take all the pupils to the funeral, so we'll have to be quick.

Where is the funeral? 'Well, at the school!' We never get a chance to learn any more, as, forty-five seconds after pulling away from the plane, we have arrived at the school. Pat looks at his watch a lot and says pointedly, 'I've got to be at the school at one o'clock.' It is now ten to one and we are at the school, but we take him at his word and hurriedly remove a thousand camera cases, twenty-four 21-inch pizzas and some fish hooks from the back of his pick-up and leave them in the lobby area of the school. Pat pulls away, literally as we are lifting the last stack of margaritas.

At this point the school caretaker with a face like an angry dog and a diamond stud in his ear leans out of the door and shouts, 'What the hell is with all this pizza? And what the hell are these?'

'Fish hooks,' we mumble, looking at our shoes and wishing we were driving back down the Dalton Highway.

'What?!' The janitor disappears in a fury of confusion. We use the lull in proceedings to film my arrival with the pizzas at the door of the school. I sneak a cheeky look at my watch. The plane taking us out of here isn't coming for three hours, and they're looking like they might be the longest hours I've ever known. At this dark moment a lesson must have finished, as a cloudburst of rowdy children, all carrying fizzy-drinks cans, comes pouring out through the door. They hop on to skidoos and tear off like a tiny chapter (a page?) of bikers dispersing into the settlement.

The school itself is quite something. Like a lot of the buildings in the settlement it's on stilts so that it sits above the permafrost. But this is a major modern construction – and huge too. Absolutely no expense has been spared on it. The classrooms are spacious and chunky and would be the envy of any school anywhere, kitted out immaculately and finished very attractively in wood – around any corner you might expect to bump into Kevin McCloud just walking off camera after a final appraising comment on how effectively they've managed to pin down the light. When one considers that every element of the building had to be flown in and constructed onsite, the mind boggles at the cost of it all.

Suddenly a cheery fellow appears and declares himself to be the principal. At last! A person who not only knows who we are but also what we are doing. We were beginning to wonder ourselves ... but, no, the principal seems friendly and unflappable. He quickly takes control of the pizzas and fish hooks situation, which is a blessing and, better still, the combination seems to make sense to him. We film a brief sequence of me handing over the comestibles and the barbs to the genial pedagogue in one of the stranger rituals of my travels to date, and he explains that he has even sorted out a member of staff for us to interview. Things are beginning to look up.

Brooks (we never discovered his surname) is the geography and PE teacher at the school and at first seems quite uncomfortable speaking to us, explaining that he also has to rush off to something at 1.15. For a small place, Anaktuvuk seems to be running on a hell of a timetable. But once we've settled in, Brooks proves rather an excellent – not to say caustic – guide to settlement life. He came to Anaktuvuk from Wisconsin some years ago and has married another teacher at the school and started a family here.

What brought him to Anaktuvuk? 'Well, I grew up in a remote part of Wisconsin, so I wasn't bothered by the remoteness here.' Yeah, but there's remoteness and then there's Anaktuvuk. 'Yeah, but you know, I love mountain-eering, snowboarding, ice hockey, fishing and I've got it all right here.' He isn't kidding. His geography classroom is lifting with expensive equipment: rows of neat brand new skates, sophisticated bows and arrows and archery targets, gym equipment of all shapes and sizes. He has got it all here. We later discover that his Anaktuvuk salary is almost double what it was in Wisconsin, which must also have played a part in the decision.

I ask where the pupils go after leaving school. Do they leave the Pass to go to university? 'Er, no, not really.' There is an awkward pause . . . 'They kind of stay here.' And what do they do? 'Well, they do all kinds of things, a bit of hunting maybe, er . . .' What sort of jobs are there in Anaktuvuk? 'Er . . .' Another pause; what's coming? If this were a Sunday evening drama, there'd be a cutaway shot of me right now catching the eye of my accomplice in a way that says 'This might be important, Sergeant.'

'Thing is, everyone gets the dividend.' What's the dividend? 'It's a payout from the oil company to all Native Alaskans.' Right. 'It's kind of twenty thousand dollars a year.' And who qualifies? 'Oh, every single Native Alaskan from the day they're born. Which is kinda great, but it means none of them really has to work.' Right, and so is everything else paid for by oil money? The school, the public buildings, the four police cars, the fire station, the airport? 'Yup.'

By the time we finish our chat, it is twelve minutes past one, so Brooks has time to make his 1.15 meeting, but he says he'd been kind of hoping we'd overrun so he wouldn't have to bother going. Instead, he takes us outside, to the hill behind the school, so we can get a good shot of the settlement. So where does Brooks go to do his ice fishing? 'Oh, there's a lake about six miles away.' What about the lake just here? I ask, pointing at the huge body of water we flew in over. 'Someone went out on it on a snowmobile five years ago and died. So we don't fish there. Nobody goes there any more.' How did that happen? 'They were drunk.' I thought it was dry here. 'Mmmm, it's meant to be, but it isn't; alcoholism is a huge problem.' Brooks looks uncomfortable but goes on. 'No one here dies of old age; it's always booze. The person whose funeral is today? She drank herself to death.' How do they get it? 'They smuggle it in. Or make it illegally. Drugs are becoming a problem too . . .' Who said it had to be dry here? 'The elders put it to the vote and the community voted overwhelmingly for alcohol to be illegal.'

We jump into Brooks's car and he drives us right across the settlement: from the dump half a mile out of the village one way to the huge fire station and water storage facility at the other end. Anaktuvuk is not a big place, but it doesn't feel like a particularly happy one either. The Alaskans who have settled here are one of the toughest races on earth. They have a proud nomadic heritage, a history of roaming freely around the top of the globe hunting caribou and moose; I couldn't swear to their ancient existence being an easy one, but it was certainly purposeful. They subsisted according to their ancient tribal rites, ruled by their elders, their religion and their traditions.

Modern Alaska has tried hard to do the right thing by these people, clearly, but in the process has thrown away – it seems to me – pretty much everything that was meaningful about their lives. They are now forced to live in a way that modern America can deal with, in houses, in streets, eating pizza and watching the game, but find themselves disconnected from their old way of life and completely at sea in the new. Their elders, who have always been their councillors and authority figures, now tend to leave the community just when their revered old age kicks in, so they can move to places like Fairbanks and take advantage of the free healthcare. And that $20k a year dividend everyone receives isn't always a blessing; it's certainly a major disincentive to the kids leaving school to make something of their lives. The oil companies are trying to do everything they can for Anaktuvuk (and presumably every other community like it), and they must be ploughing hundreds of millions of dollars a year into it. They fly in more tons of fizzy drinks than you can get your head around, they then fly in the dentists to fix everyone's mouths. They fly in the snowmobiles and the contraband booze, then they fly out the corpses to be embalmed and returned to be buried. And of course there are other problems here too. In a small isolated community like this, where everyone is closely related, inbreeding and all its myriad health complications become an inevitable issue. Suffice to say Anaktuvuk isn't exactly Utopia.

We wait in Brooks's car on the runway, willing our plane to appear in the sky. Anaktuvuk is one of the more beautiful places we've seen, but God it's a cursed one, to the extent that I even find myself looking forward to being back in Fairbanks. The pilot who eventually appears like a conquering hero over the mountaintops is a man called Todd. He's everything you'd hope for from a bush pilot: short and jolly and qualified to fly. Above all, he's extremely easy-going about having a film crew using their equipment in his cabin.

18

Nome Is Not Where the Heart Is

The following morning we fly on up to Nome in the north-west of Alaska. Nome is another old gold-rush metropolis, peopled by workers from out of town. It's rather splendid, Nome, and in the sweep of its town centre you get the feeling that it has hardly changed since the glory days of the rush. Huge civic buildings of yesteryear (nearly all of which have massive old gold pans outside their entrances like the trade symbols of medieval merchants) jockey with bustling engineering companies and colourful bars. In fact one thing Nome really isn't short of is bars. This seems to have a galvanizing effect on us for some reason I don't entirely understand – it's not that we haven't been in places with bars, and it's not that we've stayed away from bars, I think it's just that this is the first place we've been in the Arctic where there are more than two bars and the prospect of a pub crawl means we check into our hotel and head back out with unseemly haste.

We discover that the main activity in the bars of Nome (apart from some spectacularly professional drinking) is – weirdly – scratchcarding. Seven or eight huge jars line up behind the bar of every boozer, each full of different flavours of card all selling for a dollar. Every bar you walk into, the first thing you notice is the piles of discards all over the floor. At one place we go, the Polar Bar (I like what they've done there), the floor is literally knee-deep. People sit up at the bar in silence, industriously working their way through fistfuls of scratchcards and throwing them over their shoulders at a rate of about one every six seconds. It's a bloody odd sight – particularly as all the time I am there, watching hundreds possibly thousands of dollars of cards being bought, I never see more than $10 paid out.

Our hotel – our home from Nome, if you will – has the pleasant feeling of an English seaside guesthouse looking out over the sea (we're even on Front Street, which feels like a wonderfully English resort address). Only the sea in this case is the Bering. It's frozen completely solid, and there is a notable absence of piers. When seas freeze up here, they take on pleasingly similar characteristics to those they have when unfrozen; a boiling tidal sea freezes with mountainous angry ridges and troughs of dramatic ice waves, a flattish sea freezes flatly. Both, however, are marked with quite scary deep cracks that you want to get over quite quickly if you happen to be striding out offshore.

We somehow managed to drive through miles and miles of Iceland without ever stopping at hot springs – you certainly spot them all over the place thanks to the flatulent plumes of steam that parp up into the cold air at strangely random points in the landscape. But we never had time to pull over and gawp at the strange phenomenon of natural heat in the frozen wilds and, besides, we were hoping to get the chance to meet the Hot Spring as an idea in Alaska if we possibly could so didn't especially want to steal its later thunder. When you're making a programme that involves meeting people or seeing things for the first time, I find it's generally better if you don't meet them before-hand or there's something slightly phoney about your onscreen reaction. There must be a number of people dotted around the Arctic Circle who to this day wonder what was going on with that strange fellow with the bald patch who refused even to acknowledge them and then suddenly fell on them when the cameras were turning . . .

Up around Nome there are several hot springs, all of which have huge and historic significance for wildlife and people alike. Unsurprisingly they have been revered as supremely holy places for as long as human memory stretches back – and why wouldn't they be? I've already mentioned the strange animal attraction you develop towards heat in these temperatures, and stumbling across a natural source of the stuff – even if you understand every last geological detail of how it comes into being – is still a cause for wonder, love and praise. Also I suppose they must have been such distinctive landmarks in an otherwise relentless infinity of snow, ice and rock that they would make an obvious rendezvous if two groups of Early Man were struggling to think of a place to meet up for cocktails. Around the hot springs, like around oases in deserts, flora of all kinds suddenly spring to surprising life as the permafrost is not so perma after all. This in turn brings animals and thus a coherent little habitat evolves.

Unsurprisingly the prospectors of the early twentieth century were also led to the magic of the springs and overnight these sacred places of native lore, cherished down the long millennia, were 'discovered' and given names ('Pilgrim Springs!', 'Serpentine Springs!') and bars, brothels and casinos popped out like spots on a teenage chin. But the rush receded and the passing trade dwindled, and the heat came off the hot springs so that today they are by and large back to their wild state once again and now they're on land owned by powerful Native Alaskan corporations.

We take a helicopter up to the Pilgrim hot springs – about three quarters of an hour's flight from Nome – flying, as we have for so much of this adventure, over frozen hills and plains. The road out of Nome rolls on, first to its winter limit (about five miles), which is as far as the snowplough is prepared to clear between October and May. Up to this point there are several attractive houses with drives and frozen fields around them (including our

pilot Tom's house, which I'm relieved to say I compli-
mented before he confessed ownership – note to future
self: always compliment every house you fly over in a
helicopter, possibly even in cities, just in case . . .). Come
the summer, the road curls on around miles and miles of
corners and valleys, occasionally peering out from beneath
thick ice and snow to declare its presence to the view of a
passing bird's eye.

On the final approach, the springs announce themselves
not so much with clouds of billowing steam like we saw in
Iceland but simply by the presence of tall trees (well, taller
than the dwarf birches that are all we've seen for weeks),
and there in amongst the trees we see tiny splodges of dark
that muster then move with gathering pace. These are
moose. And but for the noise of the helicopter we probably wouldn't have spotted them, but our approach spurs
them into action. Next to the springs themselves is a group
of rather well-preserved derelict buildings, one – somewhat surprisingly – a tall chapel around which the others
gather in a decrepit courtyard.

We sit in the helicopter waiting for the blades to stop
spinning, staring out of the windows at this extraordinary
place. I have visited many sites of ancient spiritual significance before, most recently in Iceland, of course, but
Northumberland is positively humming with them (the
Lady's Well at Holystone, Brinkburn Priory, the Abbey on
Lindisfarne and many more! As they say on adverts), and
when you visit them you get a sense of their benign
ambience. Now I know that sounds like utter balls, but

there is often an aura about a place – when you're buying a house, for example, you get an instant sense of whether or not you like the feel of it – and here at Pilgrim Springs the atmosphere is . . . well, somewhat creepy.

It doesn't help that the derelict buildings around the old Jesuit chapel are the remnants of an abandoned orphanage. Or that the toys of the orphans – old rusty tricycles – are still peeping up through the deep snow. We find our way into what must have been the boarding house and wend our slightly anxious way up the stairs, none of us daring to be the one that turns back. Upstairs the rooms are full of jumbled cots and bunk beds for tiny people. And suddenly one's heart breaks for the poor children who were sent here following the flu pandemic of 1918, to live under the care of a Jesuit priest and a couple of nuns. In those days the only route here was three and a half hours by train from Nome to a lonely station and then two hours on by horse and cart. Once they arrived at the orphanage, this small basin of bare hilltops would be their only horizon, and the starchy priest and nuns their only parents. Tom later told us that there were many chilling tales about the orphanage that did the rounds in Nome, including one story of there being a mass grave somewhere on the site. Now obviously I've been in the bars of Nome and seen for myself how manically the regulars are prepared to buy into anything that's laid before them, but on the other hand there's no denying how dismal this place feels. Its potential as the setting for a horror story is rather too strong to ignore.

The chapel itself is completely boarded up but, with the blessing of Kevin Bahnke (our Native Alaskan guide), we climb in through one of the windows. It is rather beautiful and, like the other houses on the site, very sturdily built. The walls are panelled in painted cast iron in the chic style now favoured by Soho House clubs, the sun pours into what one might call the nave (although it only really amounts to a fairly normal-sized room in practice), but beautiful murals shine down above the altar, which remain completely undamaged after years of neglect (the great advantage of being sub-zero, as we've noted elsewhere, is that damp never really becomes an issue . . .). I'm glad there was at least one place here that might have lifted the spirits of those poor wretched inmates, but even this room could only have looked half-decent when the sun shone, and that was never going to make up for the abject bleakness of the rest of it.

Kevin and I wander around the pools admiring the fine filigree effect of the steam freezing on to the plants beside the water, crusting like gouty crystals on a toe joint. Finally we find a suitably easy pool for sloping into, so I ask if we can just take the plunge. I've brought some bathers along just in case the spirit moves me, and so not for the first time I find myself stripping off in sub-zero temperatures (this time below −25°C) and edging gingerly towards a body of water without the first inkling of what to expect.

As with the Ice Swimming in Tromsø, having made the decision to swim you have to remove your clothes as fast as possible and squelch through the snow to the water's edge. The snow and ice underfoot and between toe mean that you really have no choice at all but to proceed into the hot water, as trudging back to your pile of clothes without having warmed up would be a spectacular shortcut to frostbite. So Kevin (who never comes here without his enormous Hawaiian shorts) and I pad into the water.

I am honestly expecting something moderately tepid that might be warm in patches – it seems then (and still seems now) impossible that such a broad and shallow (maximum of three-feet deep) expanse of water could hold its heat when spread out across that cold, cold ground. How much more wrong could I have been? The water is as hot as I can just about bear. If you put your toe into a bath that temperature you'd quickly remove it and run the cold tap for a good minute. We don't have that option obviously, and so we carefully inch our way into the cauldron-heat until we reach that reckless point of no return and hurl ourselves fully in.

Then – and only then – do I see and feel the religious comfort of this place. The effect is miraculous. I feel like I have been wrapped up in my mother's arms and held tight and warm – the sheerest bliss you could imagine made all the more stark for being in that extraordinarily unprepossessing place. Little mechanical systems in my head that have been working flat out to deal with the cold suddenly find themselves on glorious holiday. I feel as if I might suddenly belch out that little electronic bleat that mobile phones make when you plug them in to recharge. I am in some fabulous state of suspension where the earth itself has taken control of me and all my workings – all I have to do is wallow and occasionally groan at the sheer pleasure of it. I see in that instant how and why the shamans came here to find their divine powers. Whole neural pathways previously given over to survival can be freed up to think philosophical thoughts. No wonder they had so much to say.

Kevin and I stay in the pool for most of an hour, talking and gently sweating as the health-giving sulphurous rill gurgles into the pool at one end and out at the other all the while. Kevin tells me about the Bering land bridge that once existed between Asia and America, allowing the migration of animals and people right across the top of the world. Of course, of course, I think, that makes perfect sense and explains why there are such strong Asian facial characteristics across the native tribes of North America and the extreme north of Europe.

When did the land bridge disappear? 'Towards the end of the nineteenth century,' is Kevin's reply. This is news to me – I had no idea it was so recent. I look it up when we get back and discover that Kevin was actually out by a couple of years. The Bering land bridge is generally believed to have disappeared between 15,000 and 25,000 years ago. But maybe an era that goes so far back before the meaningful timeframe of our history feels more recent to a Native Alaskan whose history is less pockmarked than ours. Or maybe Kevin just bunked off the day they did the Bering land bridge in history.

Kevin seems to have been much more on the ball while

studying more recent events, though. While we lightly poach ourselves in the hot springs, I learn that the Land Settlements for the Native Alaskans were brought into law by Richard Nixon in the 1970s, having festered, unresolved, ever since Alaska became a state in 1959. Neither side seemed able to agree terms until, with the discovery of oil in Prudhoe Bay in 1968 and the wafty scent of billions of petro-dollars in the air, a quick resolution needed to be found. The Federation of Natives finally agreed to keep 44 million acres and to give over the rights to their other claims for just under a billion dollars, which was duly shared out between the various regional corporations like the one Kevin works for. This arrangement explains where all the cash for the dividends comes from, and how places like Anaktuvuk are kept going. Not, it transpires, from the sheer goodness of the oil companies' hearts but from a hard-driven bargain, won when the native corporations had the US government over a barrel (or several billion barrels, to be precise). Kevin also tells me about exploration for hydrothermal power at the springs. So far they have isolated two hotspots where the temperatures are high enough to generate power that could heat the buildings and provide free energy for a decent-sized town. Maybe Pilgrim Springs' biggest story is still in front of it.

Kevin and I drag ourselves out of the springs and sit in a glorious sweaty post-bath heap that makes the gusty, tousling Arctic winds – for a space of about four minutes – the very last word in comfort. By the time we're back in our clothes, however, our core temperatures have returned to normal and our brains once again need to counter the cold rather than wallow in it. We did find the sweet spot of Pilgrim Springs but, my God, you have to dig around a bit to get beyond the Hallowe'en set of the orphanage. As we circle in the chopper on our way back to the scratchcards, the whole site disappears back into its natural context, just a fold in the scrubby hills where the furious geology of the underworld makes a sudden and unexpected call.

19

Stepping Westward

Our time in the Arctic is drawing to a close. We have one more day here before starting our slow journey home. The last trip we are making – and the last segment of the documentary – will involve a visit to an island in the Bering Straits, the icy channel that runs between Russia and Alaska. Little Diomede is right in the middle of the Straits and is separated from its neighbour Big Diomede by a mile-wide stretch of the frozen sea. Not much distinguishes one from the other apart from size (the clue's in the names). Oh and the fact that one is in Russia and the other in the US. Somewhere down that channel between the two Diomedes runs the international dateline, so although the two islands are at an identical time of day, Big Diomede, the Russian island, is exactly twenty-four hours ahead of Little Diomede.

I have to go over and over that in my head to try to make sense of it, and even now I'm not entirely sure I've got it right. But there we are. If nothing else, it's a wonderful illustration of the arbitrary frameworks we human beings impose on the world in order to make it fit our capacity to understand it. It's a bit like the strange business of maps: they're all flat whereas the world is round (I know, don't tell anyone!). The Mercator projection of the world that hangs somewhere in every school gives as accurate an account of the globe as an ironed-out tangerine peel would give of the fruit it once covered. We like thinking of the world as a chart because it's neat and metric and ordered and, above all, practical. And yet the actual world is full of wonderful anarchy, strange and poetic warps that defy such practical restraints. When pianos are tuned, for example, every perfect fifth has to be very slightly flattened because if each perfect fifth going up from the bottom of the keyboard to the top were an absolute perfect fifth, the upper keys on the piano would be out by nearly a semi-tone. We are capable of understanding our world through the bowed and irregular angles of nature, but we insist on legislating and ordering it on a neat four-square grid that doesn't really match up to the world at all. We'd take a workable fallacy over an unworkable reality any day. Part of my headspin today comes from the simple fact that Little Diomede was at the top-left-hand side of the massive world map in my classroom and Big Diomede was way over at the top right. So entrenched is my metric-taught grasp of this fact that I get an illicit thrill from the fact that

I will be seeing an island a mile away to my west that is in fact (as everyone knows!) actually several thousand miles off to my east.

Our pilot for this final excursion is Mike Kutyba, and our conveyance this time – as if to emphasize the symbolic importance of the divide of the Diomedes – is an absolute mammoth of a helicopter. It's like flying into 'Nam (by which I mean, of course, Chelt'Nam, into whose literary festival I have flown many times). I sit up front with Mike and am interested to note that he flies a course that stays over land for as long as possible and then when we leave land, he stays over the thick sea ice, only crossing the slushier edges at the very last minute. I am, I suppose, reassured by this tactic but can't help wondering what his less-than-complete faith in the helicopter's airworthiness is based on. He points out to me the low-lying cloud that is hovering up to about a thousand feet above sea level. We pull up to fly above it – 'Otherwise it'll freeze on to the rotors.' And that's bad? Mike just snorts at this. Not for the first time I reflect on how pleased I will be when we've landed safely back in Nome and I try to put to the back of my mind what a shame it would be to go up in a ball of flame on the last helicopter ride of the trip.

Little Diomede is another of these Native Alaskan settlements that like Anaktuvuk relies on pilots (in this case only helicopters can land here) to bring in everything they need. Mike outlines the plan: he is going to drop us at the helipad and bugger off. He isn't going to stick around while we film – Mike has a rule that he never switches his

Little Diomede just in case they don't start
ere he goes again with his unshakable faith in his
ine), so if you're there for anything longer than ten
minutes or, for instance, filming, which is generally better
done without a helicopter at full throttle on the edge of
shot, he prefers to drop you and come back in two hours'
time. Do we understand? (We do.)

We jump down from the giant 'copter into the coldest
conditions yet. With wind chill the −35° temperature goes
down (or up, I suppose) to around −60. This is a wind you
really can't stand in − even in full fox and seal hat − for
longer than a few seconds. As the chopper flies off, we are
instantly surrounded by a suspicious elder and five or six
teenage boys who are friendly enough but burst upon us
with manic questions about who we are, what we are doing
and what we might have brought for them. The elder
remains extremely guarded and, for the time being at least,
isn't at all keen on us setting foot off the landing platform,
let alone filming on his island.

Again and again on this trip, especially in its latter
stages, we have come across people who have been badly
treated by film crews in the past and, we later learn, so
badly misrepresented on film (the better to suit the story
that LA producers want to tell back home), that the shutters
now come slamming down at the merest whiff of a boom
mic. I like to think we've done some sturdy ambassadorial
work on behalf of our industry while out in Alaska by
being as sensitive as possible, but I don't really know who'll
benefit from that (or whether those that do will actually

deserve it). I lost count of the number of reality TV shows being filmed up in Alaska for the lower forty-eight states' general amusement, and as a proud Northumbrian who once turned on *Geordie Shore* by accident I know only too well how TV feels it can get away with treating sturdy Northerners ... I daresay tourism must benefit from all this, but I bet the people round here would cheerfully be shot of it all if it meant they didn't have to listen to one more bossy TV exec wandering around shouting into a mobile.

On this occasion we do eventually manage to thaw out the prickly elder (sounds like something Monty Don might want us to do). First by demonstrating that we have brought with us that most rare and precious commodity, respect, and then by releasing into their community our very own tame marsupial, Shane, to delight them with his melodious words, his hilarious beard and whatever combination of pizzas and/or fish hooks he has brought with him this time in his pouch.

The only shot we absolutely have to get is one of me looking out across the sound to Russia and Tomorrow. My heart suddenly flips at the thought that by the time it is lunchtime on Sunday with us (as it currently is just across the sound, seemingly inches away), I will be packing up all my furs and thermals, my chaga (don't think for a moment I left the woods without a bag of that stuff) and my outer two layers of gloves, for our four-legged journey back home (by which, incidentally, I mean it's a journey of four legs – we're not travelling back on an Icelandic pony. Even in 'fast' gait that'd be a lengthy jaunt). I am aching to be back home, to see my darling wife and be one of the family again. I have started dreaming of the smell of our boys (OK, that sounds weird, but I've been away a long time . . .) At the back of all that, though, there's also an awareness that I will actually be leaving the Arctic. I've become blissfully accustomed to saying 'Wow' up to twenty times a day, I have come to relish the strange ritual of dressing in endless layers, the satisfaction of pulling on a bespoke fox hat and feeling it do its work. Like Astrid and the Kiruna Kids, I too have come to cherish my acclimatization to this region.

I do my final piece to camera and as I'm doing it I realize that I have reached the most westerly point in the world. Yes, you could say the same, and with a clearer western horizon, on the beach at Santa Monica, or anywhere down the west coast of the Americas for that matter, but here it is literally true. I have arrived at the place where the sun finally sets. There's a lovely poem by Wordsworth called 'Stepping Westward' where he recalls a walking holiday in Scotland and a 'wildish' sunset on an otherwise dark, damp evening. It is, he ponders, a kind of 'heavenly destiny' for us to follow the sun to its setting place. Maybe through the ages we're heading west as well (like The Stranglers' heroin . . .). Which must mean that after stopping at so many frozen chapels we have finally arrived at a truly holy spot. Our journey, from Bodø right up to the other end of Russia by Murmansk, across Iceland and Greenland and

Canada, suddenly feels like a pilgrimage to this place: the page-turn of the world's diary each midnight.

We head up to the school to wait in the warmth for Mike's return, children of all ages crowding around us, all enthusiastic and polite. The tiny ones are so uninhibitedly affectionate that it squeezes your heart. They run up and hold our hands or simply smile sweetly then run away and hide. The teenage boys from the helipad are rather more raucous. They've brought with them a youngish new schoolteacher who's just arrived from the mainland for a twelve-month stint, which on the scale of things is probably up there alongside chief taster at the grouse vodka factory in terms of Jobs I Wouldn't Necessarily Rush To Do. He seems to have gone biblical hermit hairy. He has a beard that makes Shane's look like five o'clock shadow and hair like a grenade going off in a haystack. But he's an extremely genial fellow and evidently a hit with the young Diomedians.

One of the teachers passes round some hot chocolate, which is extremely welcome, and we sit in this strange cocoon of normality, a classroom that could be anywhere from Hackney to Djibouti, hung about with children's projects and safety posters, sipping our sweet drinks and forgetting for a moment that we are right on the edge of civilization. My mind can't stop wandering to this island's frozen sibling just across the ice. Big Diomede once had a settlement on it like Little Diomede's; indeed the two communities were very close and I daresay supplied each other with much needed genetic variety. However, the

Russians gave the Big Diomedians the choice of moving to Siberia or being shot (a decision I would have to spend some time over . . .). And so presumably the only evidence of life over on the bigger lump of rock now is the occasional glint from binoculars and that ticklish sense of someone's cross hairs framing you up at all times.

I've experienced several very different Arctics over the past few months, but some things have been the same wherever we've been: the raging beauty of the landscape, the soft colours of the light and, yes, now I think about it, the sense that one kind of cross hairs or another has always been hovering over us. The very act of staying alive up here requires active measures to be taken. The cold could kill you in its (and your) sleep, the icy roads might see you off at any time, as could a polar bear, or simply the oppressive ennui of life on the frozen tundra. And then it hits me like a jolt: these icy dreamlands will have me in their sights for evermore. Such is the intensity of the experience of being up here, a combination of the majestic surroundings, extreme climate and then the extraordinary *gemütlich* warmth of (most of) the people in this frozen world that I won't ever be able to shake it off – I will have to come back and drink it in again whenever I can. The beauty of this wilderness is largely down to the fact that we have left it alone, but as the earth gets fuller and warmer, and as the Arctic mineral deposits look easier and easier to get at, you've got to wonder how long it can remain un-buggered about with. Maybe even this programme I'm making is part of a stirring of interest in the region. Is the great tourism explosion in Iceland just the first sign of a more general invasion by the rest of us?

I will take so many extraordinary memories home with me from the North, not just of the places I've been but of the people I have met on the journey – from the Ice Road Truckers and their grateful message board (incidentally, you'll be glad to hear that we left $50 for Otis behind the counter – I wonder if he went for chicken puff or berry), to David and Jenna and their whiffy mukluks, to good old Børge and his bottomless cup of coffee, Ono and his scraggy dogs, Jon with his little Bodø flying club, our lovely pregnant waitress in the Lofoten Islands, even Haircut and Pass-Ag at the Downtown Hotel pool table. I have met endless fascinating people who've shown me that it is actually possible for human beings not just to live in the teeth of this forbidding climate but to thrive and be happy here.

I swirl around and drain the dense chocolate-y dregs at the bottom of my mug and stride out into the wind to catch our ride back home.

Acknowledgements

Huge thanks to Michelle Signore at Transworld, for getting the ball rolling, and to Andrea Henry, my editor, for her patience and support; her expert guidance was invaluable to this first-time writer going beyond five thousand words for the first time. Beside me all the way, like a support boat alongside a Channel swimmer, with encouragement and (figurative) hi-NRG drinks, was the indefatigable Ben Thompson – my gratitude to him. Peter Bennett-Jones and his team (Lucy and Emily) deserve my eternal and grateful thanks for all that they do for me. Thanks too to Messrs Fincham and Klein at ITV for commissioning the programme, and to Shirley Patton at ITV Books for her hard work in securing a relationship with Transworld. Jeremy Phillips and everyone at Shiver did a splendid job of putting this series together; all the production team deserve mention and thanks. Rog, our utterly brilliant cameraman, and Callum and James, our peerless sound recordists, were spectacular, and Dominic Ozanne, our sainted director, was one of the biggest contributory factors to this series being such a thorough joy to make – thanks to all of them for their magnificence.

Ultimate thanks to my amazing wife, Hannah, for keeping every plate spinning at home while I was swanning about having a high old time in the North. I know who does the harder job . . .

Picture Acknowledgements

All images have been supplied courtesy of ITV Studios unless otherwise stated. Particular thanks to Philippa Leeder.

Map © Tom Coulson, Encompass Graphics

Section One
Page 1: Marines training, courtesy of Petty Officer (Phot) David Gallagher
Page 2: Twin Prop, courtesy of Hermione Drew
Page 3: Fishing in Ballstad, courtesy of Hermione Drew

Section Two
Page 5: Hubcaps in Dawson, courtesy of Hermione Drew
Page 6: Courtesy of Hermione Drew
Page 8: Crew line-up, courtesy of Shiver Productions

Index